Topics in Autism

*R*ight from the *S*tart
Behavioral Intervention for Young Children with Autism

A Guide for Parents and Professionals

Sandra L. Harris, Ph.D. &
Mary Jane Weiss, Ph.D.

Woodbine House ◆ 1998

All rights reserved under International and Pan-American copyright conventions.
Published in the United States of America by Woodbine House, Inc., 6510 Bells
Mill Rd., Bethesda, MD 20817. 800-843-7323.

Library of Congress Cataloging-in-Publication Data

Harris, Sandra L.
    Right from the start : behavioral intervention for young children with autism /
Sandra L. Harris, and Mary Jane Weiss.
    p.   cm. – (Topics in autism)
    Includes index.
    ISBN 1-890627-02-X (pbk.)
1. Autistic children—Behavior modification.   I. Gill-Weiss, Mary Jane.
II. Title. III. Series.
RJ506.A9H269 1998
618.92'8982—dc21   98-17020
                                                    CIP

Manufactured in the United States of America

10   9   8   7   6   5

In Memory of Our Fathers
William W. Harris and William J. Coneys

And in Honor of Fathers Everywhere
Who Bring So Much Love and Energy to
Their Children with Autism

TABLE OF CONTENTS

INTRODUCTION

Parents of preschool children with autism have more reason for optimism about the future of their child than ever before in the history of this disorder. There is much to celebrate. There is also great need for caution, however. Two major issues face every family seeking treatment for their child. First, there are not enough first-rate services to meet the needs of all of the children who need early intensive behavioral treatment. In some parts of the United States there are painfully few professionals who understand autism, and in many other parts of the world resources are essentially nonexistent. As a result, many families are unable to locate adequate services for their child. Some families fall prey to service providers who are neither honest nor competent. The lack of resources is a tragedy that can only be remedied by an on-going program of education for professionals and parents alike and by public recognition that dollars spent on early treatment bring enduring economic as well as human benefits to society.

A second major issue facing families is the realization that even in the best of programs only about half of the children make enough progress to participate fully in the academic mainstream when they reach school age. The other children continue to need a great deal of educational support, although most do make more progress than they would have with less intensive treatment. This is a source of deep disappointment for many families, who understandably wish their preschool child to develop into one of those who does exceptionally well.

We have written this book to help parents become informed consumers of treatment for their child. Our hope is to educate parents about the reasons that applied behavior analysis is essential in the treatment of every child with autism, and to help them learn how to locate first-rate services for their child.

About This Book

The purpose of this book is to introduce you to the issues involved in the early, intensive behavioral treatment of children with autism and related disorders. The first chapter will introduce you to a few basics about behavioral treatment, early intervention, and the law. In Chapter 2 we will briefly summarize what the research tells us about the benefits of early intensive behavioral intervention. We will also give you a few basic principles to follow in deciding whether a program deserves your trust. Chapter 3 describes different models for early intensive behavioral intervention in autism, including home-based and center-based models for treatment.

Chapter 4 looks at one of the complicated decisions parents have to make—whether their child's program should be home-based or center-based. We will review some of the pros and cons involved in this decision making. Chapter 5 offers an overview of the curriculum that you might find in a good early intervention program. We have based this information on our own experience at the Douglass Developmental Disabilities Center. One of us (SLH) has been at the Center since 1972 and the other since 1985. Because we know it well, we will often use examples from that setting to illustrate our points. For example, in Chapter 4 the curriculum description is based on our preschool program at the Douglass School. There are, of course, many other fine programs in the country, and we use the Douglass School only as an example.

Finally, Chapter 6 offers some guidelines for parents in deciding whether any program, whether home-based or center-based, is suitable for their child. Although the chapters in this book are arranged in a sequential order, if you have a specific concern you can safely skip from one chapter to the next.

This book is intended for parents of children who have been diagnosed with one of the pervasive developmental disorders. Precise diagnosis of very young children is sometimes difficult, and for the purposes of this book it does not matter if your child is labeled as having autistic disorder, Asperger's disorder, childhood disintegrative disorder, or atypical autism (PDD not otherwise specified). Although the long-term prognosis for children in these four groups may be somewhat different, their early treatment is similar. If your daughter has Rett's disorder, her developmental course will be different than for children diagnosed with any of the other pervasive developmental disorders, and you will want to take that into account in her treatment. However, some of the information in this book will be useful to you as well.

Unless we are referring to a concern specific to one disorder, we will use the term "autism" to mean children on the broad spectrum of pervasive developmental disorders. It is a concise term that parents and professionals often use to refer to children with a variety of pervasive developmental disorders, especially autistic disorder.

Sandra L. Harris and Mary Jane Weiss
Piscataway, New Jersey

ACKNOWLEDGEMENTS

This book is the result of our many years of collaboration with one another and with a remarkable group of colleagues at the Douglass Developmental Disabilities Center and the Rutgers Autism Program. We are grateful to Maria Arnold, John Barnard, David Celiberti, Lara Delmolino, Lew Gantwerk, Peter Gerhardt, Rita Gordon, Jan S. Handleman, Barbara Kristoff, and Ellen Piccolo for all they have taught us over many years. Jill Szalony helped us with the programs for social skills. Without Jean Burton, professor emeritus in Psychology at Rutgers University, there would not have been a Douglass School. Generations of children and families owe her thanks.

Parents and children are our most important teachers. To all of the families who have honored us with the care of their children over these many years, we express our deepest thanks for their trust and collaboration in the education of their child. We know there is nothing more precious to a parent than the welfare of a child. Special thanks to Kevin and Kathleen Norris Lyons for their help. We appreciate the contributions of the many families whose advice is found at the end of every chapter in this book. Although they have remained anonymous to protect the privacy of their families, their sharing has enriched this book.

Our thanks to Phyllis Binder, Rosanna Galletley, Ilona Harris, Cheryl Howlett, Naomi Lawrence, Kathleen Lyons, Terri Morano, Kathleen Nevins, and Ramona Walsh for permission to use photographs of their children. Thanks also to Coleen Boyer, Dana Cotter, Leslie Engle, Ilona Harris, Jill Szalony, and Gary Zuckerman for permission to use photographs of themselves. We appreciate also the cooperation of countless other families who gave consent for us to use photos, but whom we could not include in this edition.

On a personal note, our thanks to Danny Weiss, who is probably the best psychologist we know! Immeasurable gratitude is extended to Danny for his limitless patience, flexibility, support, and humor. Mary Jane also wishes to thank her brother and sister for their support, and her mother who has always been a source of wisdom, courage, and strength. Sandra thanks her brother for his love, and her grandniece Emma for the joy that comes from the sheer fact of her being.

1 | An Introduction to Early Behavioral Intervention in Autism

The G Family

Tad was Grace and Allan G's second child. Their older girl, Maryanne, was five years old when Tad was born. Everything seemed to go right with Tad's early development. He was the product of a full-term, uneventful pregnancy and a relatively easy delivery. He slept well, ate well, and his early milestones such as sitting and crawling were all on time. He was an easy baby who demanded little attention, rarely cried, and seemed content to lie in his crib and gaze at the mobile above his head. Grace once commented that Tad was so good a baby he had hardly disrupted their family routines. That early picture was destined to change much too soon.

When Tad was about a year and a half old his parents began to feel nibbling concerns about him. He still had no words, not even "mama" or "dada." Although people reminded them that boys sometimes talk later than girls, they worried that he was delayed in his speech. Grace and Allan also began to sense that their initial impression that Tad was an "easy" baby might have been misleading. They realized that Tad often seemed quite absorbed in his own world and simply not interested in his family. Tad would ignore his sister's efforts to play with him, and even throw a tantrum and push her away if she persisted in trying to show him toys or to make him laugh. One of the few things that Tad seemed to find truly pleasurable was being tossed in the air by one of his parents, or even by a stranger. The other little games of childhood that his sister and cousins had all enjoyed at his age left Tad indifferent.

As he approached his second birthday, his parents became more certain that something was seriously wrong with Tad's development. He still had no speech, had started to wave his fingers in front of his eyes and gaze at his hands in seeming rapt fascination, and would often tantrum when his parents tried to get his attention. They knew this was not just normal variation among children, or the slight lag of a little boy slow to speak, but something very different about Tad. At his second birthday party Tad showed none of the curiosity and pleasure the other two-years-olds were demonstrating as they nibbled at cake, smeared frosting, and climbed on the toys. Tad simply sat to the side, rocking once in a while and watching his fingers. When the other children grew especially loud, he would cover his ears and turn away. It appeared that he had no idea he was supposed to be the center of this special day. The party was emotionally draining for Grace and Allan. As they cleaned up the debris of the "celebration" and shared their concerns, they realized they had to press Tad's pediatrician for some answers.

The G's pediatrician was concerned when she heard Grace and Allan's report of Tad's behavior. Although she herself was not certain of a correct diagnosis, she recognized immediately that Tad's behavior was very unusual for a two-year-old. She wondered whether Tad might have autism, but she had seen only a few cases in her career and did not want to jump to a conclusion about so serious a diagnosis. Rather than making the decision herself, she referred the Gs to a developmental pediatrician at the local university hospital. The Gs called the hospital's developmental clinic that same day to make an appointment for their son. Several weeks later they observed through a one-way mirror while a team of professionals evaluated Tad. Grace and Allan also answered a very detailed series of questions about Tad's development, and about their family history. Following a careful evaluation by the developmental pediatrician, a child clinical psychologist, and a speech and language pathologist on the staff at the hospital's outpatient developmental clinic, the G's received the sobering news: Tad had Autistic Disorder.

Grace and Allan were stunned by the diagnosis and had to struggle to hear the rest of the words of the diagnostic team. Their fear and sorrow filled the room, leaving little space for them to grasp more details of the evaluation. The diagnostic team realized how painful this moment was for Tad's parents. They understood that the G's would need time to absorb what they had heard that day. Grace and Allan agreed to return a few days later to meet with the team psychologist to discuss in more detail the next steps in Tad's treatment. It was a sad and anxious few days of worry and tears. Allan, who usually coped with stress by "doing something," checked the Internet and found some information about Autistic Disorder. Through that search they contacted the Autism Society of America (ASA) and that led to their local state chapter of the ASA. The bookstore at the mall had a couple of useful books. Grace went to the library and found a book on autism and its treatment that was very helpful. But, most of all those first few days they worried.

Their meeting with the clinical psychologist helped Grace and Allan begin to focus on how to meet Tad's needs. The psychologist told them how fortunate they were to recognize Tad's problems while he was still very young. He said that there was some very good research showing that many young children with Tad's diagnosis benefited from intensive behavioral intervention, or applied behavior analysis, as it is often called. This behavioral treatment could be done at home or in a school-based program. He urged them to visit several excellent schools in the area and see their programs for very young children. He also gave them information about professionals in the area who consulted to families about home-based programs.

Is the G Family Like Yours?

The G family's experience in learning about their son's diagnosis and what they went through in seeking services for him are not unusual for parents of very young children with autism. A great deal of good research on diagnosis over the past quarter century, and considerable effort to educate professionals about autism, has increased the likelihood that the family pediatrician will recognize when a child has a serious developmental problem such as autism.

In addition, there is good research documenting the benefits of intensive early intervention for children with autism.

The G family was exceptionally fortunate because they lived in a state that had many resources for children with autism. In many places in the United States and around the world they might have been advised to seek treatments that would not have been so beneficial for Tad. For example, they might have been told to try play therapy or a program placing an exclusive emphasis on sensory treatments. Neither of these approaches has documented empirical (i.e., research-based) support in the treatment of autism.

In spite of the helpful information that was available, the Gs were thrust into a complex and demanding situation almost over night. They had to deal with their intense emotional reactions when Tad was give a serious diagnosis, and almost immediately had to start searching for the right educational program for him. There was no time to catch their breath! They had to live with a mixed set of emotions. There was the pain of the diagnosis and the hope that the right program might be of major benefit to him. There was the anxiety of trying to identify a program for Tad, and the relief that there was something specific they might do for him. The turmoil was intense and family life was turned topsy-turvy by those two words–Autistic Disorder. In later chapters we will trace some of the G's experiences in selecting a program for Tad.

What is Early Intensive Behavioral Intervention?

Do not confuse early intensive behavioral intervention with the term "early intervention." Early intervention is a general term referring to services for infants and toddlers with all kinds of disabilities, while early intensive behavioral intervention is a very specific treatment shown to be helpful in treating autism. Currently the majority of early intervention programs do not offer intensive behavioral intervention. They may treat children with autism using other methods. Unfortunately, there is a dearth of good research to support these other interventions.

It may be helpful to dissect the phrase "early intensive behavioral intervention." "Early" always means beginning before the child turns five, usually before four, and preferably as young as possible. "Intensive" describes the many, many hours of treatment that are required. The term "behavioral" refers to the use of applied behavior analysis, a special kind of teaching that will be described in the next section. Finally, the word "intervention" simply means treatment.

There are several features that make applied behavioral analysis (ABA) special in the treatment of young children with autism. One is the intensity of the treatment. It should be done for at least 30 to 40 hours a week with most of the teaching being done in a one-to-one teacher to child ratio. Second, ABA is a highly structured approach to teaching. This is not a "go with the flow" or "follow the child's lead" method. Rather, it is carefully designed and follows very predictable patterns of instruction. Third, there is minimal down time during which the child is not actively learning. Brief breaks are followed by brief lessons at a rapid pace. In addition, applied behavior analysis is based on well-studied principles of human learning and is designed to capitalize on the capacity of children to benefit from proven methods of instruction.

Legally, the general term early intervention applies to services for infants and toddlers with disabilities from birth through the age of two years. Children three and older are considered part of the educational system rather than the early intervention system. However, in the autism field it is very common to hear the term "early intensive behavioral intervention" used to describe treatment services for any child up to school age. We will use the term early intensive behavioral intervention to refer to the treatment of any child with autism who is below kindergarten age.

What Happens During a Teaching Session?

As explained in the section above, a technique known as applied behavior analysis is at the heart of intensive behavioral intervention for young children with autism. To help clarify what is meant by "applied behavior analysis," here is a brief overview of what goes on during a teaching session.

Initially, teaching sessions are done in a space that has been arranged for this purpose. It might be a corner of a child's room, a section of the classroom, or another reasonably quiet and distraction-free setting where the teacher can control the level of stimulation. Usually there will be a small table and chairs, although sometimes a child may work on the floor or in a beanbag chair. The structure should be determined by the child's needs.

These early sessions rely on a method called Discrete Trial Instruction (DTI). DTI is one of many instructional techniques used in Applied Behavior Analysis. It is a critically important teaching method because it provides a very clear and simple framework for learning. With DTI's clear instructions and consequences, a variety of behaviors can be taught while children with autism are in the earliest stages of learning. DTI is the most efficient and effective method of instruction for these early lessons. Other ABA techniques become relevant as a child progresses in the mastery of skills.

A teaching session using applied behavior analysis involves a series of requests, tasks, or questions that are posed to the child. Each item to be taught is broken down into simple components in order to maximize the likelihood that the child will be able to respond. First the teacher gives an instruction such as "Do this" while she models a simple gesture such as clapping hands. Then, in the early trials, she reaches over, grasps the child's hands, and helps him clap. Gradually, she fades (phases out) this "prompt" until the child is responding independently to the command "Do this." She also gradually mixes hand clapping with other previously learned imitations such as foot stamping and head patting. After a few correct responses, each one of which is followed by praise and a small reward, she gives the child a brief break, saying "Go play." Then, after 30 seconds or so, she summons him back for a few more trials. Gradually, the number of trials between breaks increase and the breaks grow longer.

After each correct response the child is rewarded or "reinforced" for his good work. This reinforcement might include a tiny bit of a favored food, a few moments of play with a desired toy, or a sip of juice. It also includes words of praise such as "Great job," "Super work," or "Way to go." This praise is delivered with great enthusiasm.

In addition, the teacher keeps a record of how many correct versus incorrect responses the child makes. She uses these data to determine when to move on within the program. Because ABA does not rely on subjective opinions about progress, ABA is often referred to as a "data-based" technique.

The Skills Taught Using Applied Behavior Analysis

The skills to be taught using applied behavior analysis include the full spectrum of activities essential to the child with autism. These range from self-help skills such as dressing and face washing to very complex social skills involved in play with other children. Speech, receptive language, and academic readiness skills such as matching, using a pencil, number concepts, and letter recognition can all be taught using these methods. Although these tasks may sound complex, they can usually be broken down into small units that are easier to teach than the whole skill at once. For example, teaching speech may begin with reinforcing any sounds the child makes, then gradually helping the child make those sounds more and more like a desired sound. The sounds can then be attached to objects as the child begins to label with simple words like "ball."

In addition to being used to teach new skills, applied behavior analysis can be used to help children with autism learn to control disruptive behaviors such as tantrums, stereotyped behavior like body rocking or hand waving, and noncompliance. Chapter 5 describes a typical curriculum in more detail.

Who Needs Early Intensive Behavioral Intervention Services?

Every young child who is diagnosed with a pervasive developmental disorder including autistic disorder, childhood disintegrative disorder, and pervasive developmental disorder not otherwise specified (sometimes called atypical autism) should receive early and intensive behavioral intervention services. This treatment should begin as soon as possible after the diagnosis is made. Although the specific components of treatment will vary depending on the child's needs, each of these children should be receiving services. As discussed in the next chapter, the research documenting the benefits of these treatments is substantial, and the risks of failing to intervene before school age are very serious. One does not wait to see if a child will "outgrow" autism.

We cannot rely on a child's intelligence as measured by an IQ test to predict how he or she will respond to these teaching methods. It is certainly an advantage if your child is able to cooperate with this testing and shows signs of normal or near normal intelligence. However, we know many very young children who were initially classified as having mental retardation who responded well to teaching and are now functioning in the normal intellectual range. Furthermore, as Tristam Smith and his colleagues have shown (1997), even children with pervasive developmental disorders and severe mental retardation do better when they have intensive treatment than when they do not. Do not let your child's tested IQ score deter you from using applied behavior analysis.

Although we do not yet have research showing exactly what happens in the brain of a young child with autism who receives intensive teaching, we believe there are enduring changes for the better in how their brains function. It appears that with good teaching their brains are at least partially able to compensate for whatever the deficit was that gave rise to their autism. This potential for change, or "plasticity" as it is sometimes called, is one of the reasons we cannot assume that a child who tests in the mentally retarded range before treatment will remain in that category after treatment. We do not yet know which children will respond best to treatment and which will not. It is therefore essential that every child have access to this opportunity.

As mentioned in the Introduction, intensive behavioral intervention can be helpful to children who have been diagnosed as having any of the disorders under the broad heading of pervasive developmental disorder (PDD) according to the criteria of the American Psychiatric Association in their *Diagnostic and Statistical Manual.* This includes autistic disorder, childhood disintegrative disorder, and atypical autism. It also includes Asperger's Disorder. However, because children with Asperger's Disorder are not as obviously impaired as children with other forms of PDD, they are sometimes not identified until school age. As a result, these children may not be recognized as needing services in the years before kindergarten. If you have a child with Asperger's Disorder who is below school age, by all means seek early intensive behavioral intervention services for him.

What about Older Children?

Parents of older children with autism who have not received early intensive intervention often wonder whether it is too late to benefit their child. Applied behavior analysis is helpful for people with autism, regardless of their age. However, the most substantial changes in a child's developmental path are likely to occur during treatment at an early age. Perhaps because the brain loses some of its plasticity as children grow older, the gains for school-aged children and adolescents are more modest. In spite of this limit, it is important to know that behavioral treatment at any age can be highly beneficial. Every child deserves the best education possible.

The ways in which ABA methods are used typically differ based on a child's age. For example, unless they pose very unusual management problems, older children usually work in small groups and focus on different instructional content than younger children. The methods of ABA are used to teach skills appropriate to the child's age. This can be seen in the choice of reinforcements (rewards) for good work. A very young child might work for a reward of chocolate pudding or tickles, and an older child might work for pennies to buy a treat of her choice. Thus, the content and context may differ, but the teaching methods are based on the same scientific principles of human learning.

How is Intensive Behavioral Intervention Related to Early Intervention?

Today, generic early intervention services are considered essential for children with a wide variety of disabilities. Some children enter an early intervention program when they are tiny infants, particularly if they are known to have suffered traumas during the birth process or were born with disabilities such as Down syndrome that are evident from birth or very early in development. By contrast, children with autistic disorder, Rett's disorder, or pervasive developmental disorder not otherwise specified (atypical autism) may not be diagnosed until they are approaching their second birthday. In the case of Asperger's disorder or childhood disintegrative disorder, the diagnosis may be made later still. For a child like Tad G, who has a condition on the spectrum of autism, the early months may be uneventful and parents may be quite unaware that their child will need special services.

Once an infant or toddler is identified as possibly needing early intervention services, he is evaluated to determine whether he qualifies to receive early intervention services at public expense. Typically, a team of professionals with different areas of expertise will observe and test him to see whether he has significant developmental delays or is considered at risk of having delays. If the evaluation team finds significant delays, the infant or toddler is declared eligible for early intervention, and qualifies for a host of benefits and protections under the federal Individuals with Disabilities Education Act (IDEA), Part C.

Early intervention services may be provided in several different settings, including in the home, a school, a hospital, or a special clinic. One common way to describe early intervention programs is based on their location—in the home or outside of the home. Programs provided in the home are called "home-based," while those done in hospitals and other agencies may be called "center-based." Often early intervention programs combine these two approaches, with the center-based program providing direct service to the child and also teaching the parents what to do at home.

The specific services a child receives in an early intervention program will depend upon his needs. These services can include speech and language therapy, physical therapy, interventions to stimulate cognitive (intellectual) development, and so forth. Physicians, psychologists, educators, dieticians, physical therapists, occupational therapists, and social workers may all become involved in working with the child in an early intervention program.

Families who enroll their children in early intervention programs receive an Individualized Family Service Plan (IFSP). This is a document that families and professionals jointly develop. It specifies the short-term and long-term goals that parents and professionals would like to see the child achieve, as well as the treatment methods and therapies that will be used to help the child reach his goals, the assessment procedures that will be used to determine whether goals are met, and information about support to be provided to the family. This is similar to the Individual Educational Program (IEP) for a school-aged child, but is focused on the needs of very young children and their families.

Early intervention programs rely upon parents as active members of the child's treatment team. This is because it is considered essential that the child's learning be consistently supported throughout the day, and not just in treatment sessions. Parents are typically taught many of the treatment techniques being used by the professionals who serve the family. Parents may then carry out treatment sessions just as a professional might, or they can supplement the work of the professional, working to ensure a carry-over from the treatment session to the child's daily life.

For children with autistic disorder or a related condition, early intervention program services typically focus on speech and language services, cognitive and social development, and behavior management. If there are problems with motor control or other specific deficits, suitable services would also be offered to meet those needs. However, very few early intervention programs offer intensive behavioral treatment, and if you want those services for your child you must shop for them. Again, early intervention is not the same as early intensive behavioral intervention! If a program does not meet your child's needs, you should look for resources that are appropriate. Don't settle for an inadequate program.

The next few sections explain how to find out what types of services your local early intervention program offers for children with autism, and offer suggestions as to what to do if the local program does not routinely offer intensive behavioral intervention for young children with autism.

What Does the Law Say?

The civil rights movement in the United States not only had a direct impact on the rights of people of color, women, and adults with disabilities, but also was part of a process that resulted in improved educational opportunities for children of all ages who have disabilities.

Your child's right to educational services varies with his or her age. The dividing line for services is the third birthday. Children younger that three years are served by the early intervention system and those three years and older by the educational system. It is important to know what the federal legislation says about the education of children at different ages so that you can ensure your child is getting the services to which he or she is entitled.

From birth through two years of age, your child's right to services is based on the Infants and Toddlers subsection (Part C) of the Individuals with Disabilities and Education Act (IDEA). That law gives federal assistance to states to support comprehensive and broadly based early intervention services. These services must meet a variety of criteria, including the use of a multidisciplinary team to conduct the assessment, and the creation of an individual treatment plan for each family (called an Individualized Family Service Plan or IFSP). All states provide treatment services for infants and toddlers. No matter where you live in the United States, you and your infant or toddler have the right to services. However, while some services such as evaluation and assessment are free, the state may charge for direct intervention (e.g., therapies and specialized instruction) on a sliding fee scale.

After a child reaches the age of three years, his or her educational needs are covered by Part B, the portion of IDEA that concerns school- aged children. This legislation assures your child of the right to a free (at no cost to you) and "appropriate education" in the "least restrictive setting" necessary. It stipulates that an Individualized Education Program (IEP) be developed for your child, detailing in writing what services provided in what setting will be provided your child as part of his "appropriate education." Since understanding what is meant by an "appropriate education" in the "least restrictive setting" is crucial to ensuring that your child benefit from his educational program, let's examine those terms in more detail.

The law allows a great deal of latitude for interpretation of what constitutes an appropriate education for every child, and you as a parent have many rights in making decisions about your child's education. For example, appropriate special education can go beyond academic instruction to include support needed to help your child master daily living skills and to enhance his social and emotional development. An extended school year longer than the 180 days typical in most school systems, home support, or residential treatment may all be deemed "appropriate" for some children. Because the federal legislation does not dictate specific treatment for specific disorders, there is room for debate about what is "appropriate" for a child. You should know, however, that "appropriate" is usually not interpreted by early intervention and special education programs to mean "best."

Similarly, there can be differences of opinion about what setting is "least restrictive," or permits a child with disabilities to have the maximum contact with normally developing peers. Included in a typical class in a public school at grade level? Placed in a special class in a public school? A private special education class? Home-based instruction? Any of these may be least restrictive for some children.

The only way to be certain you are acting in your child's best interests is to know the law in some detail. Your local school district must provide you with a written copy of all of your legal rights concerning your child's education. In addition, you can get a copy of your state's special education regulations from the state department of education. You are also entitled to have access to every report and other document that has been written about your child. As a parent, nothing should be kept secret from you. You must also give your consent prior to any evaluation of your child. If you do not agree to an evaluation, the school must go to a due process hearing in order to over-ride your decision. In addition, you can request a due process hearing if you and the school disagree about other aspects of your child's program, including the least restrictive setting, the services provided, and whether or not assistive technology is provided for your child.

In sum, a series of federal laws have been enacted by the Congress of the United States which ensure that your child has the right to appropriate educational services from birth to age 21 years. For parents of young children with autism, however, most of the challenges lie not in finding some form of treatment for their child, but in finding *appropriate* treatment. Early intervention and preschool staff may not always have the needed expertise in the treatment of disorders on the spectrum of autism, professionals may disagree with parents about what constitutes appropriate treatment, or a community may lack programs that are proven to be effective.

Although IDEA has proved helpful to many families, it may not be sufficient to ensure that you will be able to obtain the services your child needs. Many families have had to resort to lawsuits, or the threat of such suits, in order to obtain the program their child requires. On the other hand, some early intervention programs and school districts are remarkably helpful, and some have well-trained staff to serve families. Your own experience will hinge on where you live and the specific people with whom you deal. Expect to be served well, but be prepared to act assertively on your child's behalf if need be. Sometimes

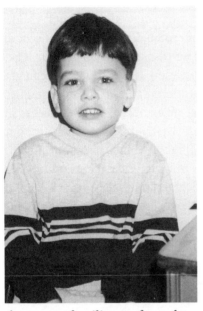

that action may include contacting a lawyer well versed in disability law.

One problem some families of children with autism encounter is reluctance from their funding agency to support a home-based rather than a center-based program. There are at least two major arguments to raise on behalf of home-based services. One is that many very young children are normally at home until they begin kindergarten. Related to this is the notion that many families prefer to have their young child at home and under close parental supervision until the child is of school age. Chapter 4 discusses in more detail the pros and cons of home-based and center-based treatment.

Working with Your School District Or Early Intervention Agency

If you suspect or know that your child has a disorder on the autism spectrum, contact the office of your local school district or early intervention agency and speak to someone who can arrange an intake evaluation for your child. These professionals should work with you to evaluate your child's needs, develop an educational plan, identify potential placements, and help you make a placement decision. Not only do they have the legal obligation to serve your child after she turns three, they also are often caring people who want to do what is best for children. Many families receive a compassionate, highly intelligent, and helpful response from their local school district.

If your child is under three, your local early intervention program is responsible for your child's education. Although some of these agencies are responsive to the highly specialized needs of children with autism, many of them are not. In our experience, the public schools tend to be more alert to these special needs. As a result, you may need to assume much more initiative (and expense) for your child prior to the age of three years. If you are very fortunate, you may live in a school district that recognizes that money spent on the intensive treatment of a two-year-old will often save thousands of dollars later. Recognizing this cost-efficient (not to mention humane!) intervention, they may serve your child even before she turns three. See our discussion in Chapter 4 of how to enlist the help of a reluctant school district.

Be open to professional input. Try to find professionals you trust and work with them collaboratively, but always keep your highest priority in mind—your child's welfare. Remember that no one can be as loving and devoted an advocate for your child as you can.

What about Other Treatments?

This book is designed to help parents understand the importance of using applied behavior analysis in treating young children with autism, and to help them set up or find an appropriate program for their child that uses ABA. However, many different approaches have been tried in the treatment of autism, and your school district or early intervention program may very well use something other than ABA in working with young children with autism. What should you do if you encounter this situation?

It is important to find out whether a program is based on research proving that it is effective. There are a few long-standing, highly reputable programs that are not, strictly speaking, ABA programs. One example is the TEACCH program (**T**reatment and **E**ducation of **A**utistic and Related **C**ommunication Handicapped **CH**ildren), founded in North Carolina in 1972 by Eric Schopler and his colleagues. This program makes extensive use of structured teaching methods, but Schopler stresses that it differs in important ways from applied behavior analysis. Among these differences are the number of hours of instruction and the instructional ratio (number of children working with a teacher). The TEACCH program also places an early emphasis on independent task completion and following picture schedules.

In addition to programs such as Division TEACCH which have studied the impact of their methods on children, there are also many programs which are not data based (i.e., based on research findings). These programs should be approached by parents with a great deal of caution. As discussed in Chapter 2, the most extensive research on the treatment of preschool children with autism has been done using applied behavior analysis. Because it is the best-studied method and the one we use in our own work, it is the intended focus of this book. Parents who wish more information about the structured teaching methods employed at TEACCH should see the chapter by Catherine Lord and Eric Schopler (1994) listed at the end of this chapter. They can also contact Division TEACCH at the University of North Carolina Medical School in Chapel Hill for more details.

Every quality program should be able to explain in detail their teaching methods and conceptual framework. In Chapter 6 we discuss how to evaluate a potential placement for your child. Although our criteria in that chapter focus on ABA programs, they will also be useful in evaluating other approaches.

Parents Speak

When I first heard the word "autistic," my son was 18 months old and running around the pediatrician's office. At first I thought the doctor was totally out of her mind. Who knew anything about autism? I certainly didn't. Yes, he was doing odd things and yes, he was developmentally delayed, but autistic—no! All kinds of thoughts were running through my mind on the drive home from her office. Through my tears I wondered how the most beautiful baby boy I had ever seen could possibly have this horrible disorder. I felt I was handed a life sentence. I wondered if he would ever play baseball, have friends, talk, and call me mommy. I wondered if I would ever dance with him at his wedding. Finally, I began to read and read and I haven't stopped yet.

૭૭

I still remember that drive home from the neurologist's office as though it were yesterday. Bang! Your kid has autism. Here is a list of schools where you can take him. Maybe he said more, but I didn't hear it. All I heard was your kid has autism and I thought it meant he had no future. I must have cried for a week.

૭૭

My wife and I knew before the doctor even said anything that Tom probably had autism. I had been to the library and done a lot of reading. We figured it out before the doctors said anything. So, when the news came we were ready.

૭૭

I still can't get over it. How could this child, smaller than a minute, have so much wrong with her brain? I wasn't going to let that happen. We started right away with treatment. She was only 30 months and so we had people come to the house to work there. The first few weeks she hollered for hours. But, after that she settled down and seemed much calmer. It got so she would hug the therapist and then run and get the little chair.

૭૭

In retrospect I think that every doctor who saw him knew what they were looking at, but they referred us on to the next doctor on the checklist without telling us. It would have saved us a lot of time if they had told us their suspicions.

My wife and I were ushered into a doctor's office and the door was closed. The doctor handed each of us a copy of a thick, computer-generated document, sat behind the desk, and began reading from her copy of the diagnosis–word for word, typos and all–without looking up at us.

I felt a deep sorrow for the first two years or so. When I was happy I wasn't as happy as I used to be; when I was sad I was a lot sadder than I used to be. It was the first thing I felt when I woke up in the morning and the last thing I felt at night when I went to sleep.

⌒◯

We took our son to a major child development center for a comprehensive evaluation. When they said the "A" word it was like being told it was incurable cancer. It was terrifying, confusing, and heartbreaking. Our search for answers began the next day with my husband's visit to the local library.

The things that helped us the most in beginning the work with our son were: 1. Getting a clear, direct, and blunt diagnosis of Autistic Spectrum Disorder; 2. Finding Catherine Maurice's book *Let Me Hear Your Voice;* and 3. Beginning a program of Applied Behavior Analysis and speech therapy quickly.

⌒◯

At his 18-month check-up he was seen by my pediatrician's practitioner, who reassured me he was just a late talker. I began asking all the young mothers in my neighborhood about their children, and they too said boys talk later than girls. Thinking that my son's lack of language and increasing odd behaviors were just his personality, I felt fairly confident there *was nothing wrong.* Meanwhile, his eye contact diminished, his love of rocking and swinging became obsessive, he often acted as if he were deaf, and would occasionally laugh hysterically at nothing apparent. *At his second birthday all the guests played in our backyard while my son wandered off examining the vinyl siding on our house.*

The pediatric neurologist's explanation of my son's diagnosis was both shocking and perplexing. I was so convinced my son was merely language delayed that the word "autism" hit me like a cold shower. The information in the library devoted to autism was sparse and bleak.

References

Maurice, C., Green, G., & Luce, S.C. (eds.) (1996). *Behavioral intervention for young children with autism: A manual for parents and professionals.* Austin TX: Pro-Ed.
    A good book on treatment for young children with autism. It includes a chapter by Mark Williamson on legal issues in funding programs. If you run into problems getting the services you want for your child, take a look at his chapter. In general, it is a fine and useful book.

American Psychiatric Association (1994). *Diagnostic and statistical manual of mental disorders. 4th ed.* Washington, DC: Author.
    If you want to read the criteria professionals use to diagnose Pervasive Developmental Disorders, go to the library and look at this book.

Smith, T., Eikeseth, S., Klevstrand, M., & Lovaas, O.I. (1997). Intensive behavioral treatment for preschoolers with severe mental retardation and pervasive developmental disorder. *American Journal on Mental Retardation, 102,* 238-249.
    This is the article we mentioned on the benefits of applied behavior analysis for children who have pervasive developmental disorders and severe mental retardation.

Lord, C. & Schopler, E. (1994). TEACCH services for preschool children. In S. L. Harris & J. S. Handleman (Eds.) *Preschool education programs for children with autism* (pp. 87-106). Austin TX: Pro-Ed.
    See this chapter for more on Division TEACCH.

2 | Does Early Intensive Behavioral Intervention Work?

The G Family Checks the Facts

His family often teased Allan G about his passion for the Internet. But, when Tad was diagnosed with autistic disorder, and the family had to search for resources for Tad, Allan's passion became a valuable tool. Grace and Allan wanted to be certain they found the right treatments for Tad. It was important to learn which of the many approaches they heard about were actually helpful, and which were just fads or money-making efforts by people who might not have Tad's welfare at heart. A search on the Internet for listings under the topic of "autism" led them to a series of home pages describing resources for people with autism. But the information on these pages was often contradictory and confusing to a parent new to autism. Grace and Allan realized that people who based their conclusions solely on their own personal experience, not on research or objective evaluations, had written some of what they were reading on the net. Other people's personal experience was important in thinking about their decisions, but Grace and Allan wanted more information before they made choices for Tad.

A book that both Grace and Allan found very helpful in deciding how to help Tad was Let Me Hear Your Voice: A Family's Triumph Over Autism, *by Catherine Maurice. The description of how Dr. Maurice had sought treatment for her own children with autism helped Grace and Allan settle on applied behavior analysis as their treatment for Tad. Later, they would also discover an edited book by Maurice and her colleagues Gina Green and Stephen Luce (1996) that had a great deal of information about applied behavior analysis in the treatment of autism.*

During their Internet search, Allan and Grace had also noted that the term "applied behavior analysis" kept coming up in chat room discussions. They also realized that the name of a UCLA psychology professor, Ivar Lovaas, was often mentioned in the same sentence as applied behavior analysis, or "ABA," as they soon learned to call it. Lovaas was a well-recognized scientist, and his work seemed like a good place to begin.

A visit to the university library led them to an important publication by Professor Lovaas, which described his very impressive success in working with young children with autism. It was a technical article, and not easy for a layperson to read, but the general message was clear. Dr Lovaas reported that his behavioral treatment was very effective for a number of the young children in his study. This was the most hopeful note Grace and Allan had found in their search for help. As they read more about ABA they realized that Dr. Lovaas had been vital in initiating this line of research, and that a number of other people were now following up on his impressive results with important findings of their own. The fact that other research supported the work of Dr. Lovaas added even more weight to his findings. The good news was not limited to one center. Grace and Allan wondered if there might be programs in their own state that offered similar services.

One evening, the Gs were reviewing what they had found on the Internet, in the library, and in the special education section of a local bookstore. Grace pointed out to Allan that applied behavior analysis was the only treatment method they had found which had good research to back it up. Although some of the other methods they had read about were interesting and sounded good on paper, there was not much research supporting them, and it was impossible to tell if they really worked. The Gs decided that they were not willing to take a chance with Tad's welfare and that they would use the only method that seemed to be "tried and true."

Once they knew the kind of treatment program they wanted for their son, their next task was to choose the best program for Tad.

To do so, they would have to decide which of several programs claim-
ing to use the techniques of applied behavior analysis was using the
methods most effectively.

What Does the G Family Search Mean for You?

It is not unusual for parents of young children with autism to learn a great deal about treatment options on the Internet. However, the problem with information from the Internet is that there is no quality control. Anyone can write anything. It is impossible to know which programs that are described on the Internet are good and which are not. You cannot tell who is honest and who wants to make a buck or attract attention to him- or herself. The reader has only the individual opinions of strangers whose children may or may not resemble her own.

Although the Internet serves a valuable function in sharing information, it is less helpful in ensuring that this information has been carefully evaluated. The buyer must beware! Recognizing this limitation of the Internet, Allan and Grace went to the library to look up information in professional journals. At a large bookstore that had a section of books on special education they found several paperback books that were very helpful and that were written with parents in mind. That reading was helpful to them in reaching a decision about their son's treatment. However, not everyone is prepared to plow through professional journals or buy books. Rather than turning to the library or a bookstore, some parents prefer to ask the opinion of a trusted professional. Regardless of how you get the facts about your child's options, it is important to ensure that you know what you are doing when you select your child's program.

It is probably also a good idea to check things out with more than one source. For example, if you read something on the Internet, look it up in a book as well. If one professional makes a suggestion about a treatment, ask another her opinion too. Your local autism society, the national Autism Society of America, and brochures provided by various treatment programs may also be helpful. After a while, you will learn who you can trust, but until that happens, keep a skeptical attitude.

In this chapter, we describe the research on the behavioral treatment of young children with autism. We will also suggest some questions you can ask when you evaluate the claims that people make about any treatment method. You don't need a doctorate to do your own research! This chapter is intended to help you be a well-informed consumer of professional services.

What Happens to Children Who Receive Early Intensive Behavioral Intervention Services?

The very good news is that many children who receive intensive behavioral services at an early age do very well in that treatment. Some children make substantial gains in intelligence, social skills, and adaptive behavior. However, there are also many other children whose benefits are limited to modest changes. Even as we celebrate the improvement in our ability to treat autism, it is important to recognize that some children make limited gains, and they continue to need highly specialized services. While you work toward maximum benefit for your child, you must remember that the degree of change is very individual. Some children will make rapid progress, and other children will make slow and modest gains. We often cannot tell before treatment starts which children will make quick gains and which will progress more slowly. Still, it is important to put maximum effort into the treatment of every child. We need to know that we have done the best that we can for each child regardless of her long-term outcome.

Because of the very human tendency to celebrate our success, it is often easier for professionals to remember and focus more on their best outcomes when talking about their programs, and to put less emphasis on the children who make slower, more limited progress. People also want to make families feel better

and sometimes they do that by playing down the sad fact that not every child achieves the best possible, hoped-for outcome through applied behavior analysis.

As a parent, your most important objective will be the gains *your* child makes—not the best a school has produced, or the average for children in a given class, or children with autism in general. It is the outcome for your son or your daughter that matters most deeply and personally. In order to be realistic about your child's outlook you need to know the facts about the full range of possible outcomes from a treatment program. Then, you can work toward the best, but understand that there are no guarantees for your child, or any child. No one knows when a child walks through the door how he is going to respond to treatment. If someone promises you huge gains, run fast in the other direction.

The Lovaas Study

What has research found about children with autism who have participated in intensive applied behavior analysis treatment from early childhood? To answer that question, we turn first to the most important study in the field, the research Professor Ivar

Lovaas did at UCLA. In 1987, Lovaas published a paper in a professional journal that was to have far reaching influence on the field of autism. In this paper he reported on his work with 38 young children with autism. One of the requirements for being included in the study was that at the beginning of treatment the children had to be younger than 40 months of age if they were mute, or younger than 46 months old if they had echolalia (parroting back speech). The children were divided into two groups. One group of 19 children, called the "Intensive-Experi-

mental Group," received at least 40 hours a week of one-to-one treatment for at least two years. The other group of children, called the "Minimal-Treatment Control Group," had not more than 10 hours a week of one-to-one instruction during the two-year period.

Before the children started treatment and again when they were between 6 and 7 years old, a number of measures of their abilities in different areas such as intelligence and adaptive skills were made. The treatment procedures used by the therapists in Lovaas's study were based on the principles of applied behavior analysis. In the earliest phase, the instructors attempted to reduce the children's disruptive behavior such as their tantrums, to increase their compliance with instructions, to teach them to imitate what other people did, and to teach them simple toy play. In addition, family members were taught the behavioral methods being applied by the staff so that they could be part of the treatment team. The second-year curriculum focused on expressive and abstract language and learning how to play with other children. In their third year of instruction, children were taught to express emotions, worked on pre-academic readiness skills, and learned how to acquire new skills by watching other children engage in a behavior (sometimes called observational learning). When they were ready, children were moved into regular preschool classes, and then into regular educational classes whenever possible.

What Professor Lovaas learned from this study continues to influence the education of young children with autism more than a decade later. He found that nearly half (47%) of the children in the intensive treatment condition were functioning at a normal level intellectually, and were in regular education classes when they were re-evaluated at 6 to 7 years of age. Only one child in the minimal treatment group made the gains in intelligence and educational achievement found in the intensive treatment group. The results of Lovaas's study suggest that 10 hours of intensive teaching is not enough to make the difference for children with autism, but 40 hours or more of this instruction can lead to major changes for some children. It does not tell us what 30 hours or what 20 hours a week might do, only about the difference between 10 and 40 hours.

In addition to studying the children during their early childhood, Dr. Lovaas and his colleagues kept in touch with them over the years. In 1993 Lovaas and his colleagues John McEachin and Tristam Smith described their long-term follow-up of the children who had participated in the Intensive Experimental Group. At an average age of 13 years, the intensive treatment children who had made early gains continued to hold their own. In fact, 8 of the 19 children were now described as "indistinguishable" from other children their age on measures of intelligence and adaptive skills. It is very heartening to know that the progress they made in the preschool years was not lost by the time these youngsters were entering adolescence. It is also important to note that none of the children who had been in the control group had achieved this level of functioning.

In sum, Lovaas's research shows that intensive behavioral intervention at an early age enabled nearly half of his young participants to achieve essentially normal intellectual and academic functioning. The much poorer performance of the comparison group supports the argument that these changes were not simply the result of getting older, going to school, and so forth. The highly specialized treatment was necessary to bring about major change.

Other Studies on Early Intensive Behavioral Treatment

Although Dr. Lovaas's study is the most scientifically rigorous report of the benefits of early intensive behavioral intervention for children with autism, it is not the only study to find clear benefits from applied behavior analysis. For example, there is a report from the Princeton Child Development Institute in New Jersey, a program for children with autism directed by psychologists Patricia Krantz and Lynn McClannahan. See Chapter 3 for a brief description of their program. Krantz, McClannahan, and their colleagues, Edward Fenske and Stanley Zalenski, followed the progress of nine children who began intensive behavioral intervention before 60 months of age, and nine who started treatment after 60 months of age. Their results showed that the children who started treatment before they were 5 years old had a better outcome than those who started later. This study highlights the importance of beginning treatment at an early age. Waiting until a child with autism is ready to enter kindergarten is much too late to begin treatment. Although older children benefit from treatment, they do not typically show the benefits of children who start when they are very young.

At our own program in New Jersey, the Douglass Developmental Disabilities Center, we tested the intelligence and language of 9 young children with autism when they first entered our preschool and then again a year later. Our children made an average 19-point increase in intelligence on a standard test of IQ, and an

8-point increase in language performance on a measure of expressive and receptive language after one school year. These data, taken in conjunction with other studies, bolster the notion that early, intensive behavioral intervention makes a measurable difference in a child's performance. There is a brief description of our program in Chapter 3.

Stephen Anderson and his colleagues at the May Center for Early Childhood Education in Boston provided a blend of intensive home-based and center-based teaching for preschool children with autism (Anderson, Campbell & Cannon, 1994). Their program included a socially integrated preschool class for children who were ready to benefit from that experience. Among the first 26 children who participated for at least one year, 14 (54 percent) went on to a regular kindergarten, 2 (8 percent) were enrolled in resource rooms in their home school district, and 10 (38 percent) went to segregated classes in private schools. Anderson and his colleagues note that many of the children in the regular kindergarten classes needed extra support such as an instructional aide.

Similar findings were reported in Australia by Jay Birnbrauer and David Leach (1993), who provided intensive early behavioral intervention for nine children. Four of these children were described as approaching normal functioning after two years of treatment, while only one of five control children had made significant progress.

Taken as a group, these several studies all provide encouraging support for the potential value of using intensive behavioral treatment for young children with autism.

Thinking about Research

This chapter is intended to give you the skills to be your own judge of scientific research. As the parents of a child with autism it is vitally important that you know how to evaluate the claims on which your child's treatment is based. There are many unsubstantiated claims in the field of autism. You need to know who stands on solid ground when she makes claims about a treatment and who does not. Not everyone who gives you bad advice wishes to deceive you; they may simply be ignorant about the best treatments for autism. There are, however, some people who probably care more about taking your money than helping your child. Regardless of their motivation, some people are not operating in your child's best interests, and the task of protecting her falls to you. Be a questioning, critical consumer.

Table 2-1 | A Primer of Common Research Terms

Adaptive Skills: Skills such as self-help, play, and social behaviors that help the child adapt to the demands of the environment.

Comparison Group: This term is sometimes used to describe a treatment condition that is used as a contrast with the "experimental" treatment under study. For example, if it has been shown that one treatment works well, that proven treatment might be used as a comparison for a new treatment that is being developed. Children in the comparison group would get the proven treatment and children in the experimental group the new treatment.

Control Group: In a research design, the control group is sometimes given no treatment or sometimes given a different treatment than the "experimental" group. A control group is used to show that common factors such as the passage of time, being in a classroom, or receiving adult attention are not the reason for the change in the child's behavior. Sometimes the term control group is used to describe a "comparison" group (see above).

Experimental Group: The experimental group is exposed to the treatment procedure under study. Their performance is contrasted with people in a comparison group (see above) or control group (see above) to learn if there is any advantage to being in the experimental condition.

Experimenter: The experimenter is the person who conducts a study. For example, Professor Ivar Lovaas is the experimenter who

Table 2-1 summarizes some of the vocabulary you can use to think about research and Table 2-2 provides a list of questions to ask about research studies.

What Does the Study Show?

The first question to ask about an intervention that is suggested for your child is whether there is any research showing that it does, in fact, do what its supporters claim and whether that re-

did an important study on the use of applied behavior analysis for treating children with autism.

IQ: The term "IQ" is an abbreviation of the words "Intelligence Quotient." An IQ is a measure of a person's intelligence on a test that has been designed specifically for measuring IQ. For children with autism, these tests are usually given individually by a highly skilled school or clinical psychologist trained in this kind of testing.

Participant: A participant is a person who takes part in a research study. Some people use the term "subject" to mean the same thing. Participants may be in either the experimental or control groups (see above). In a good study, participants do not usually choose which condition they will join. Instead, they are assigned randomly.

Replication: Replication means repetition. A replication of a research study is a repeat of that study. Often replications are done in new places by people other than the original researcher. That is called an independent replication and when it finds pretty much the same thing as the original study, we feel more confidence in the original finding.

Treatment: A treatment is what the experimenter does to the participant (see above) to try to bring about change. For example, a treatment might be the use of applied behavior analysis for six months or the use of a drug.

search was any good. In good research there is a comparison between two different experiences in order to find out if the new treatment works. Some research compares what happens when one group of children receives the treatment (the experimental group) and a second group has no treatment at all (control group). However, these days it is often difficult to find parents who are willing to withhold all treatment from their child and just hang

---

Table 2-2 | Some Questions to Ask about Research

1. What claims are being made about this treatment?
(e.g., the treatment improves speech, decreases behavior problems, prepares children to enter kindergarten)

2. Is there research to support the claims being made?

3. Who took part in the research?
(e.g., diagnosis, age, gender, IQ, speech of the children)

4. How did the experimenters measure change in the children? (e.g., educational placement, IQ, speech development, adaptive skills)

5. Were measures of skills made both before and after treatment? (If only made after, it is impossible to know how the child would have done before treatment)

6. What did they do to the children during the study?
(Is there enough detail to tell what happened?)

7. Who did the treatment? (e.g., teacher, psychologist, undergraduate assistant, speech and language specialist, special education teacher, physician?)

8. Has there been a replication?
(Have other scientists repeated the finding?)

9. Does this study apply to my child?

around waiting for a few years to see what happens! In addition, we know children rarely if ever "outgrow" autism, and early studies have shown that children who receive minimal treatment make few gains. As a result, it is common for studies on the treatment of autism to compare two different treatments rather than comparing one treatment to an untreated control group. For example, there might be an experimental treatment group and another group which participated in the standard special education curriculum offered in the community.

Is There Enough Information?

As you evaluate the information being offered to you about a treatment, ask yourself how much detail is provided about the treatment procedures used in the study. That detail will help you decide if the treatment matches your own child's needs. Was the treatment done one-to-one with one adult and one child or was it done in a group? If it was done in a group, is your child ready to work in a group, or does she need one-to-one help? Were there normally developing peers in the class or only children with autism? What skills did the teacher in the study have? Does the treatment program where you want to enroll your child have staff with training comparable to that of the people who did the work in the study? How well does the kind of information taught to children in the study match the needs of your child?

How Did They Decide the Children Changed?

Another question to ask is how the investigators measured change in the children. There are many possible ways to evaluate a child's progress. These include changes in intelligence (IQ); changes in adaptive skills such as being able to get dressed independently or to buy an item at the store; changes in academic skills such as reading, math, and writing; improved use of expressive and receptive language; and so forth. The child's educational placement might also be used to measure change. Did the children enter a regular classroom? A special education class? One problem with using class placement as a measure of outcome is that school systems differ in their expectations for when a child is ready to be fully included. Some schools will integrate every child in a regular class regardless of the degree of disability, while others are reluctant to do so. That can vary even within a state. We find some schools in New Jersey are very ready to take children in their inclusive classes when they graduate from our preschool, but other school districts want to put comparable children in a special class. In addition, a child may be in an inclusive class with varying levels of support. At one end of the continuum, this support can involve a full-time classroom assistant whose full effort is devoted to the child with autism. Under somewhat less supported conditions, there may be a "shadow" who oversees the child's performance but only intervenes when essential, and who may work with a group that includes the child with autism and her peers as well. Finally, a child may be placed in a typical classroom with no special assistant assigned for support. So, class placement by itself is not a sufficient measure of outcome.

How Do These Children Compare to Mine?

You should find out about the particular children who were in the study. How do they compare to your child? Consider such factors as the average age, IQ, diagnosis, and whether or not the children had any language. We know there is a lot of variation in children who are given a diagnosis of one of the pervasive developmental disorders. Even within a category such as autistic disorder or Asperger's disorder there is variation. Differences in outcome reported by studies may sometimes be the result of those differences. If the children we include in our research sample are older or perform differently on a test of intelligence than those in another person's study, that difference could account for differences in our ultimate results. If children with better skills before treatment do better after treatment, it may not mean that the treatment was more effective, but only that people who start with higher skills end up with higher skills. Be very careful to explore who the children were who were part of the study. Remember that the rich get richer and bright children with autism are likely to make greater gains than those who are less bright.

Can the Findings Be Replicated?

You will hear the word replication used sometimes in research jargon. It simply means repeated. It is important that researchers in other places be able to replicate or repeat the findings that come from one scientist. When a study is replicated, the scientific community has even greater confidence in it than when one person has done the research in only one setting. For example, the fact that other people have reported findings that support the work of Dr. Lovaas increases our confidence in applied behavior analysis.

What about Treatments That Cannot Be Studied?

Be wary of people who claim that their treatment technique for autism cannot be studied. Sometimes that claim is used as a way to evade the responsibility of doing research. In other cases the claim may be made because they recognize that their methods may not stand up under careful scrutiny. If a procedure is useful, there should be a way to measure the benefits.

Taking Part in Research

There is a lot of research going on to improve our educational methods for children with autism and to better understand what causes the various kinds of pervasive developmental disorders. If you and your child are asked to participate in one of these studies, look carefully at the credentials of the person who invites you into the study. Does this person have the necessary scientific background to conduct the research? If the person is a graduate student doing research under supervision, does the professor have the skills to ensure the work goes well? How will the investigator evaluate your child's progress and decide whether your child is benefiting? If the study is going to take a significant amount of your child's time, it is especially important that you have enough details to be certain it is a good study that has a fair chance of helping your child.

When in doubt about a study, ask questions. Also, remember that you can say "no" to any study that you do not believe is in your child's best interests. Be very skeptical of someone who tries to pressure you into participation or who promises you benefits that seem unrealistic. You should be given a written description of the study and be asked to give your written consent to participating. If you are not offered that information, you probably do not want to be part of the project.

All of these cautions aside, it is through good research that we have made so much progress in the treatment of children with autism. Dr. Lovaas's work hinged on the generosity of 38 families who allowed their children to be part of his project. What Ivar Lovaas and those families did stands to be of personal benefit to you and your child. If you can help a good scientist do good work, we hope you will do so.

Summing Up

A number of scientists in different parts of the world have shown that early intensive behavioral intervention can be of substantial benefit to many children with autism. The research suggests this intervention should begin at an early age and be very intensive in nature. If someone offers you a non-behavioral treatment, they should be able to show you data from a well-designed study indicating that their method performs at least as well as intensive behavioral treatment. If you use that as your measuring stick, you will be able to make good judgments about what is in your child's best interests.

Parents Speak

He needed help and he needed it now. In most all my readings, early and intensive therapy was very important. I read about Lovaas and his research with children using applied behavior analysis and the good results he was getting. After reading many articles and books, ABA kept coming up. I decided this was the way to go and I wanted to try it. I want my son to reach his full potential and I am going to do everything in my power to see that he does. Through friends I met in the early intervention program I went to, I found out about the home-based services offered at a nearby center. I got in touch with them and began a home-based program. My son was 27 months and we started with 2 hours a week and grew to 28 hours by the time he started school at age 3.

I'm a history professor and I do a lot of reading. So when we found out Rob needed therapy, I read a lot and asked a lot of questions before we started him on applied behavior analysis. I needed to be certain this was the right thing to do. There were lots of people making a lot of claims. One of the things I liked when I talked to the director at the program where Rob goes is that she didn't make any promises. She said they would work very hard with him and with us, but that she could not make any promises. I liked the fact that she was honest with us. The fact is, he has made pretty good progress, but it hasn't been magic. He still has a long way to go.

You might say my son is one of the miracle children. He has made fabulous progress in the last two years. This fall he is going to a regular kindergarten full-time. I thank the Lord and a wonderful group of teachers for that. But I see other children who started when he did who have not done so well. It breaks my heart for their parents. I know it must hurt them when they see how well Rob has done and their child has not. I try not to talk about him too much with them.

∽

I just didn't know what to do after we found out about Allison. We were lucky to have a good doctor who knew what to tell us. She sent us to the school district and they were wonderful. They found a program for Allison and she has made good progress. I'm not much of a reader, but the way they explain things to us, I don't have to be.

∽

We observed several schools in operation before deciding which was the right one for our son. Applied behavioral analysis, especially in its earliest phase, can be hard for a parent to watch. It has it origins in behavior modification, and it isn't the way parents want to teach their child. But we understood that if "normal" methods could have worked with our son we wouldn't be looking for a special school. Our son was enrolled at the age of 2 years, 10 months at a private placement at our own expense. The school district continued his placement and picked up his expenses when he turned three.

∽

You should choose a program that is data-based. Any claims of success are only useful if controlled experiments are done on a relatively large sample of children. One child benefiting from a particular remedy is not a reason to pursue it. Many hundreds of children benefiting, however, as is the case with ABA, is certainly worth pursuing.

References

If you want more information on the studies mentioned in this chapter here are the references to the original studies on which our descriptions are based.

Anderson, S., Campbell, S., & Cannon, B.O. (1994).The May Center for Early Childhood Education. In S. L. Harris & J. S. Handleman (Eds.), *Preschool education programs for children with autism* (pp. 15-36). Austin, TX: Pro-Ed.

Birnbrauer, J.S. & Leach, D.J. (1993). The Murdoch early intervention program after 2 years. *Behaviour Change, 10,* 63-74.

Fenske, E.C., Zalenski, S., Krantz, P.J., & McClannahan, L.E. (1985). Age at intervention and treatment outcome for autistic children in a comprehensive intervention program. *Analysis and Intervention in Developmental Disabilities, 5,* 49-58.

Harris, S.L., Handleman, J.S., Gordon, R., Kristoff, B., & Fuentes, F. (1991). Changes in cognitive and language functioning of preschool children with autism. *Journal of Autism and Developmental Disorders, 21,* 281-290.

Lovaas, O.I. (1987). Behavioral treatment and normal educational functioning in young autistic children. *Journal of Consulting and Clinical Psychology, 55,* 3-9.

Maurice, C. (1993). *Let me hear your voice: A family's triumph over autism.* New York, NY: Knopf.

Maurice, C., Green, G., & Luce, S.C. (Eds.) (1996). *Behavioral intervention for young children with autism: A manual for parents and professionals.* Austin, TX: Pro-Ed.
> This book includes a useful chapter by Psychologist Gina Green on evaluating research.

McEachin, J.J., Smith, T., & Lovaas, O.I. (1993). Long-term outcome for children with autism who received early intensive behavioral treatment. *American Journal on Mental Retardation, 97,* 359-372.

A good journal to read to keep up with new research developments in autism is:

Journal of Autism and Developmental Disorders. You can get information about subscriptions from Plenum Publishing Company, 233 Spring St., New York, NY 10013.

3 | Models for Serving Children and Parents

Choosing a Program

After deciding to use a treatment program based on applied behavior analysis, Grace and Allan still had choices to make. There were several different programs for very young children with autism in their community and each structured their services somewhat differently. The Gs knew they were fortunate to live in an area where they could choose among programs, but they also felt a responsibility to make the best choice for Tad.

To prepare themselves for their visits to the preschool programs, they requested brochures from each of them. They also went back on the Internet, to the bookstore, and to the library to see what people had to say about the various behavioral treatment approaches they were encountering. What a range of choice they found! One program offered integration with normally developing peers from the first day a child with autism was in school. Another program began its work right in the family's living room. Yet another program had a classroom where each child had an individual tutor providing one-to-one instruction in a school setting. That same school also had an integrated classroom where peers learned alongside of the children with autism, but they did not place children with their normal peers until they had the benefit of one or two years of individual work. There was a classroom in a public school, one at the university school, and yet another in a private school.

The time had come for Grace and Allan to see the programs for themselves. Since they were making a vitally important deci-

sion for Tad, they both took time off from work to tour the facilities in their community and to meet with the professionals who would be serving them. When they expressed their perplexity about the differences among the programs to the director of the university program, she nodded sympathetically. All of the programs the Gs were visiting used applied behavior analysis as the basis for their instruction. But each had a different model of how to apply the procedures. She added that some of the programs probably were more rigorous in their application of the technology than others. Those differences might not be evident in the brochures the programs provided. The Gs would have to select the program that made the best sense for their son, and they would have to ask enough questions to make a fully informed choice. It was not an easy task for a parent.

How Do Your Choices Compare to the G Family's?

The Gs were fortunate. They lived in an area that was blessed with a wealth of resources for serving children with autism. There were public school programs, private school programs, and a university program. There were service providers who would conduct treatment in the home and programs located in schools and other facilities. Although all of them described themselves as "behavioral," some were more faithful to that description than others. This range of services reflects the fact that we do not yet have enough research data to be certain about which models of service delivery are the best, or whether one model is in fact better than another. As a result, the Gs, like countless other families, must trust their own judgement.

Models of Intervention

This chapter describes some of the common approaches to the use of behavioral techniques in early intervention for children with autism. We will use specific well-known, highly respected schools as examples of these programs. These programs are located all around the United States and vary greatly in their structure. But they also have common features that make them all excellent. They are not, of course, the only excellent programs available. There are many programs that serve children with autism well; we happen to be most familiar with the ones we talk about here.

Common Features of Excellence

The common features that tie very good early intervention programs together are as important to know as the features that make them different. There are areas of focus that appear again and again in the descriptions of model programs. These include such factors as a rich ratio of adults to children, opportunities for integration with normally developing peers, careful planning for the transition from the specialized program to a more normalized program, opportunities for family involvement, and a well developed curriculum. It is these common features, summarized in Table 3-1, that you can look for when you evaluate specific programs for your child.

Table 3-1 | Some Common Features of Excellent Preschool Programs

- Rich Ratio of Adults to Children
- Provision for Interaction with Normal Peers
- Systematic Transition to New Settings
- Support for Family Involvement
- Well-Developed Curriculum
- Sophisticated Knowledge of Applied Behavior Analysis
- Well-Trained and Well-Supervised Staff
- Knowledgeable Administrators

Number of Adults

It is not uncommon for programs to offer a one-to-one ratio of adults to children during the child's first year or two of instruction. Although not every excellent program does this, most do. When they do not offer one-to-one teaching, the rationale is well-developed and not simply the result of insufficient resources.

Access to Normal Peers

At some point in treatment, most excellent programs include an opportunity for contact with normally developing peers. The ways of doing this vary, with some programs offering integrated placement from the child's first days, and others delaying this placement until the child has mastered what they regard as prerequisite skills. Some programs have children with a range of disabilities and include the children with autism in classes for children with other challenges such as learning disabilities or communication delays. Regardless of when they offer integration with normally developing children, excellent programs recognize that for most children with autism this exposure in the preschool years is crucial if the child is to achieve full educational integration.

Planned Transition

Administrators of excellent programs have learned that without planning carefully for moves from one class to another, or one school to another, the child will suffer. They all therefore make special provisions for working with the teachers who will receive the child in his next placement and for ensuring that the child has the skills needed in the new setting. For example, this process may involve phasing the child into the new classroom during the spring so that he is ready for that class the following fall, doing a careful study of the expectations that are held for children in the class, and ensuring that the child has those skills before the move is completed. The excellent programs will usually offer to follow up as a consultant to the new teacher. It is also common practice to send a well-trained adult with the child to oversee the transition into the new setting.

Supporting Family Involvement.

Although parents are important in the education of any child, this is especially true for children with autism. We know it is essential that parents be able to support the teaching that goes on in the classroom. Most parents can become very skilled in behavioral teaching, but they do need the opportunity to practice these methods under the direction of an experienced trainer. All excellent programs recognize the crucial role played by parents and solicit their full involvement. These programs also recognize that, although their teaching staff is expert in behavioral technology, parents are experts in the behavior of their child. It is the combination of these two sources of expertise that will create the best possible outcome for the child.

A Well-Developed Curriculum

The skills to be taught to a child and the sequencing of that instruction are not a matter of random choice. An excellent pro-

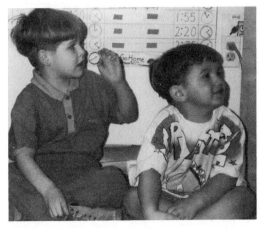

gram should have a well-developed curriculum that includes detailed instructions to teachers about how to teach the specific lessons that are selected. This curriculum is usually carefully sequenced, with an appreciation of the order in which skills need to be learned. In addition, skills are broken down into their many component parts and taught systematically. The features of a well-developed curriculum are discussed more fully in Chapter Five.

Some Exemplary Programs

The programs described in this section are excellent examples of their model. That does not mean they are the only programs that adopt that particular model, nor that they are the only excellent ones. We selected these programs either because of their excellent national reputation or because they are ones with which we are familiar. Not being on this list is not a negative reflection on a program. There are countless other excellent choices around the country.

A Public School Program:
The Montgomery County Public School System
Preschool for Children with Autism.

Autism is a relatively low incidence disorder that requires highly specialized resources. As a result, creating specific classrooms that serve an entire school district can be both cost-efficient and maximize the likelihood of having many well-trained individuals on staff. That is the general philosophy proposed by educator Andrew Egel and his colleagues as part of a federally funded model demonstration program for preschool children with autism. The model classrooms were located in Montgomery County, Maryland, and the county continued the program when the grant ended. Each classroom serves six children and has a full-time teacher, two full-time instructional assistants, and three part-time assistants. This staffing allows for the children to spend most of their time in student/teacher ratios of 1:1, although teachers also provide instruction in groups (2:1 to 4:1) during parts of the day. Related services such as speech, occupational therapy, and physical therapy are available as needed. Inclusion for the Montgomery County program occurs primarily with children in Head Start and kindergarten classrooms located in the same building. This arrangement allows the children with autism to move flexibly between the classes based on their needs. Family involvement is considered integral to the program.

A University Based Program: Douglass Developmental Disabilities Center.

The Douglass School is a program for children with autism based at Rutgers University. It includes three classes for preschool-aged children. The "Prep" class provides one-to-one instruction for six children. The "Small Group" class is composed of six children with autism with three or four staff. This class helps the children make the shift from a one-to-one ratio to working in small groups with other children with autism. In "Small Wonders," the integrated preschool class, six children with autism and seven normally developing peers share a classroom and the attention of four or five adults. There is only a small amount of one-to-one teaching, with most work done in small or large groups. A speech-language specialist is assigned half time to each preschool class. Parents are provided with training in behavioral techniques. There are regular home visits by support staff to develop home programs. Parents attend conferences at the school along with the full professional staff to share information and make plans for the child. Transitions from class to class and from the Douglass School to the next placement are carefully planned and usually involve several months of systematic skill building.

A Private School:
The Princeton Child Development Institute.

Located in Princeton, New Jersey, the Institute is a private special education school serving children and adolescents with autism across the age spectrum. A significant number of the students are of preschool age. Typically, a staff member works with one or two children at a time. The preschool does not occupy a self-contained classroom. Rather, the children make many transitions each day from one room to another, from one staff member to another, and to different activities. The rationale underlying these many changes is to maximize the child's opportunities to transfer skills to new environments. After children have mastered important prerequisite skills at the Institute, they are transitioned into more normalized settings with typical peers. This may begin with a day camp or playgroup and then move toward membership in a regular kindergarten or first grade. Family involvement is tailored to the needs of each family.

An early intervention program, opened in 1997, serves children who are 28 months of age or younger at enrollment. In partnership, parents and professionals provide 15 hours of center-based intervention and 20 hours of home-based intervention per week.

A University-Based School:
The Walden Preschool.

The Walden Preschool is a program for preschool children with autism based at Emory University in Atlanta, Georgia. The model used at Walden is different from that of the other programs described thus far. A ratio of one adult to three children is typical with a lead teacher and four or five assistants. The emphasis in the Walden program is on social integration, with children with autism and their normally developing peers being part of the same classroom from the early days of the child's enrollment. There is a strong emphasis on teaching the children how to interact with one another. Effective integration also requires careful planning by the teacher and thoughtful arrangement of the classroom and the materials. The Walden program relies heavily on incidental teaching as opposed to more highly structured discrete trial teaching. In incidental teaching situations, the teacher tries to create interesting settings that will attract the child's attention and then capitalizes on the child's interests to convey information. For example, if a child picks up a truck, the teacher might comment on its color or shape and ask the child a simple question. She might then encourage the child to push the truck to the garage. In a discrete trial format, the teacher structures the materials and lesson, rather than following the child's lead. The Walden staff encourages parent involvement and provides support for parents in learning the necessary skills. Like the other behavioral programs described in this chapter, the Walden program systematically assesses the children's progress.

A Home-Based University Service: Rutgers Autism Program.

Home-based instruction has become increasingly popular in recent years since Ivar Lovaas demonstrated the power of this intervention for benefiting young children with autism. The Center for Applied Psychology at Rutgers, The State University of New Jersey, offers one such program. Under the direction of clinical psychologist Mary Jane Weiss, the staff travel to the homes of individual families around the country to provide training seminars called workshops. These initial workshops are one, two, or three days in length, depending on the level of training of the family. During these intensive consultation sessions, the parents and other people working with the child are taught techniques based on applied behavior analysis that are appropriate for the child. The family recruits their own instructional team. Often, team members are interested undergraduates, and the parents supervise their work with the child. Families are encouraged to schedule 40 hours a week of instructional time. As the child progresses through the program, the focus of instruction moves from the home to a nursery school or kindergarten where social and academic readiness skills can be refined.

Who Are the People Who Will Serve Your Family?

A variety of professionals may be involved in the treatment of your child. Table 3-2 summarizes information about the credentials and roles of some of the most commonly encountered professionals. The following discussion offers a bit more detail about the role of each professional group listed in the table.

Physicians

Your first professional contact about your child's autism was probably with the pediatrician or family practitioner who takes care of your child's overall health. These medical specialists are physicians who have completed medical school and done specialty training as well. It is not uncommon for a pediatrician or family practitioner to refer parents to a specialist who has more experience with developmental disorders in order to obtain a diagnosis from an expert. One common referral is to a pediatric neurologist. This physician has training in both neurology (study of how the brain works) and pediatrics, and specializes in disorders of the nervous system that occur in children. Another common referral for a diagnosis would be to a developmental pediatrician. This is a pediatrician who specializes in problems of development. Another medical specialist who might have identified your child as having a pervasive developmental disorder is a child psychiatrist. This physician specializes in mental disorders of children. All three specialists would usually have considerable experience in recognizing autism.

Physicians are valuable in making the initial diagnosis of a pervasive developmental disorder. They can also re-evaluate your child over time to assess the progress he is making. If your child

Table 3-2 | Professionals Who May Serve Your Family

Applied Behavior Analyst. An applied behavior analyst is a person trained in the theory and application of principles of learning. People who use this label may have educational credentials ranging from none at all to a doctorate. It is therefore important to ensure that an applied behavior analyst has the essential skills to work with your child. See our comments about "Home Consultants."

Physicians. Pediatricians, family practitioners, child neurologists, developmental pediatricians, and child psychiatrists are among the specialists who can provide medical services including diagnosis of the pervasive developmental disorders, medication for seizures or behavior problems, and on-going support for your child's health. Each of these medical specialists has an M.D. degree and post graduate training in his or her specialty.

Psychologists. Clinical and school psychologists may provide services to your child including evaluation, consultation to parents and teachers about management of behavior problems, and supervision of the use of behavioral treatments. Psychologists have at least a master's degree and often a doctorate in their specialty.

Teachers. Special education and early childhood education teachers who serve your child have at least a bachelor's degree and often a master's degree in education. They will also be licensed or certified by the state. Teachers are in charge of the classroom in which your child is placed. The teacher will decide on the programs to be used in teaching your child and will supervise the assistants who work in the class.

Speech-Language Specialists. Speech-language specialists have at least a bachelor's degree and often a master's degree. They may also have a specialty certificate showing their competence. A speech-language specialist is often part of a child's treatment team in a school setting.

Home Consultants. Home consultants are people who come to the home of a child with autism to set up and supervise a behavioral program for the child. Consultants can have any academic degree or none at all. Because there are no laws about credentials or degrees required for this role, the quality of people who offer these services is highly variable.

needs medication, develops a seizure disorder, or has some other medical problem, a physician will be central in that treatment. However, intensive behavioral intervention is not a medical treatment and a physician does not administer it. You will be referred to other specialists for that care.

Psychologists

Clinical and school psychologists are often involved in the care of children with autism. Clinical psychologists usually have a doctorate (Psy.D. or Ph.D.) in psychology and have done a full-year psychological internship. There are some clinical psychologists with a master's degree. Clinical psychologists specialize in the diagnosis and treatment of psychological disorders. Some of them are experts in the assessment and treatment of autism. School psychologists may have a doctorate or a master's degree. They are trained to work in schools and have special expertise in the assessment and education of children. Most school districts employ school psychologists to evaluate children, consult to teachers, and help parents find placements.

A psychologist may play an important role in evaluating your child. This might include administering special tests of your child's adaptive functioning and testing his intelligence. In addition, psychologists are often called upon for consultation when a child is posing behavior problems or does not seem to benefit from treatment. Some psychologists work directly with children with autism or train parents in behavioral techniques. They may also conduct support groups for parents or siblings of children with autism.

Teachers

A teacher may be at the heart of your child's treatment. Teachers have at least a bachelor's degree and may have a master's degree in education. All states require that a teacher be certified or licensed by the state as qualified to teach. This may include a specialty credential in special education. Being a certified or licensed teacher does not ensure that a teacher has expertise in treating autism. It is important that any teacher who is working independently with your child have supervised experience with children with autism.

A teacher may be the person who identifies the skills to be learned by your child and teaches these specific lessons to your child. Typically, the teacher of children with autism has one or more assistants who work under his or her supervision in the classroom, implementing the programs written by the teacher. Because the

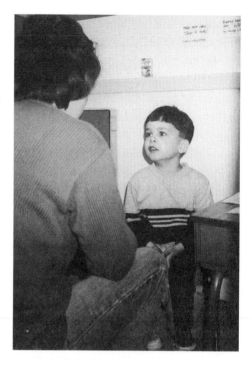

teacher's role is so vital to your child, it is important that you feel confident about the skills this person brings to the classroom.

Speech-Language Specialist

Variously known as speech-language pathologists, speech therapists, or speech-language specialists, these individuals usually have a master's degree and may have certification from the American Speech-Language-Hearing Association to document their expertise. This special credential is called a Certificate of Clinical Competence in Speech-Language Pathology. If you see the letters CCC-SLP after a speech therapist's name, it means he or she has met high standards of professional competence. Speech therapists can have a variety of specialties. Any speech therapist who works with your child should have had supervised experience in working with children with autism.

Speech and language intervention for children with autism is probably most effective when the teacher and the speech-language specialist collaborate closely. For example, at the Douglass School our speech-language specialists spend many hours a week directly in the classroom. They run language groups, work alongside of the teacher as full partners, and help the staff implement language goals. Like teachers, speech-language specialists will play a central role in your child's treatment.

Other Professionals

Other professionals may also be involved in your child's treatment. A physical therapist, who specializes in helping children with gross motor problems, may provide services if your child has problems with mobility. A school nurse may administer medication a physician prescribes. Some programs employ occupational therapists to help children with specific sensory problems. Social workers may run parent support groups and provide home support.

Paraprofessionals

In addition to the professional staff, there are often paraprofessional staff who work with the children. These individuals,

whose educational backgrounds vary, are trained to carry out specific tasks under professional supervision. For example, a classroom assistant or assistant teacher may conduct teaching sessions with your child, implementing the programs written by the teacher. Many paraprofessionals become highly skilled in their work. At the Douglass School many of our assistant teachers are people with bachelor's degrees in education or psychology who are working while they continue to go to school for a master's degree. They are usually highly intelligent and devoted people who are very effective. However, there is no credential required in most settings to become a paraprofessional, and you need to be certain that the people who work in your child's program are well trained and well supervised.

Home Consultants

There are currently no regulations concerning who can provide home-based consultation to parents of children with autism. As a result, a number of people with various levels of competence have "set up shop" offering their services to families. Some of these folks are superb and some may do more harm than good. Sadly, we are aware of children who appear to have been harmed by a consultant who did not know how to create a coherent program for the child. As we have suggested at other places in this book, it is therefore essential that you select a service provider very carefully.

Someone who works independently as a consultant to families should be well trained in the principles of applied behavior analysis. Their background should include an in-depth knowledge of applied behavior analysis, a sophisticated understanding of the procedures used to decrease disruptive behavior, a detailed understanding of autism, and a well-developed teaching curriculum. A master's degree or a doctorate in one of the appropriate professions, including psychology, education, or speech, would be important, although there are some people with less education but many years of applied experience who offer good services. A formal educational degree by itself is not insurance that a person has the necessary know-how. It is essential that their training include the skills just described. This knowledge should not be based solely on reading books or sitting in class. It is important that the person have extensive hands-on experience teaching preschool-aged children with autism under the direct supervision of someone who is expert in that work. If a consultant does not have a formal educational background in applied behavior analysis you need to ensure he or she has sufficient training to be able to handle all of the many complexities that arise in educating a child with autism. Check their credentials very carefully. When in doubt, shop around.

Some home consultation agencies employ people with bachelor's degrees who work under the supervision of individuals with advanced training. That system can work well if there is an arrangement to ensure close supervision of their work. Find out who is supervising the person who will be coming to your home, and make sure the supervisor is competent and will have an active role in overseeing the work of your consultant. For example, at the Rutgers Autism Workshop Program none of our staff go on home consultations alone until after they have first done many, many visits with a senior staff member. Initially the new staff member observes the senior person, and then gradually he or she starts to take responsibility for some aspects of the visits. Before the junior person is allowed to go to a home on his or her own, the supervisor will have observed complete visits during which the staff member took full responsibility for the consultation. Even new people with advanced degrees go through that procedure. After they are allowed to make independent visits, staff still meet weekly with their supervisor to review programming concerns. Videotape reviews are incorporated into supervision, and senior staff join consultants on their visits on a bimonthly schedule.

In Sum

Intensive applied behavior analysis is used in a number of different settings. In the absence of good research comparing these various models of service delivery, parents have to use common sense in choosing among programs. When you evaluate a program, be certain you understand such things as the ratio of adults to children, the kind of access children with autism have to normally developing peers, how children are aided in the transition to new settings, and how parents are trained in behavioral methods. If you are contracting for home-based services, pay special attention to the credentials of the person who will serve your family, and to the supervision available to staff within the agency.

Parents Speak

It was really rough in the beginning. My son would be crying downstairs and I would be crying and praying upstairs. I wondered if I did the right thing. He was so young to have to go through this torture. But as the weeks passed and the therapy increased, we began to see results. You live and die by what the therapist tells you after each session. It was amazing! Little things he couldn't do before he started to do. I then knew we were on the right road.

I don't consider myself a very religious person but I do go to church on Sunday and I do pray daily. I feel God has put certain people in my life that led me to where I am today. It is so important when you're dealing with this disorder that the right people come into your life to help you. My advice to other parents is to seek outreach services with schools that are well known in the field of autism.

இ௦

One of the first things that struck me when we walked into the school was that everyone was busy with kids. They all seemed to know what they were doing. When we watched through the one-way mirror, I was really impressed. There was one adult for every child. And so much energy. I've never seen adults with so much enthusiasm and warmth. The kids loved it. You could tell they were happy. That helped me make up my mind.

இ௦

After the interview I prayed a lot. I knew we had found a place where Danielle would get help. They said they had to wait to be certain there was an opening. I kept my fingers crossed. We had watched the preschool class with all the normal kids and the ones with autism. I had a hard time telling them apart. I just kept hoping she would be there some day. The miracle is that she finally made it. I don't know what her future will be, but she is doing great right now.

༄

Our son is one of the children who have moved very slowly. He had two years of one-to-one teaching. First he had a year at home and then a year in school. He has made some progress, but he is still very autistic. Next year he will be too old for the preschool and we are looking for the right class for him. He is probably always going to need a lot of help. I knew there were no guarantees, but I kept hoping my son would be one of the lucky ones. It isn't easy.

༄

Overall, in spite of the effectiveness of ABA, it is a bit heart-wrenching to teach your child this way. This is, after all, just a highly refined version of teaching tricks to a dog. But at least in some cases, and in our son's case, it somehow also teaches the brain how to think.

References

The program descriptions in this chapter were based primarily on information in a book edited by Jan Handleman and Sandra Harris. This is a readable paperback that parents as well as professionals find useful.

Harris, S.L. & Handleman, J.S. (Eds.) (1994). *Preschool education programs for children with autism.* Austin, TX: Pro-Ed.

Home-Based Versus Center-Based Programs

Who Should Teach Our Child?

In their search for services for Tad, Grace and Allan spoke with several families who had hired independent consultants to come to their homes to create educational programs for their child. In each of these families, the child's mother had decided to stay home full-time in order to supervise her child's education. One of these mothers, Alice M, described the process at great length to Grace and Allan. After Mrs. M learned that her daughter had autism, she heard about home-based services, and decided to follow that path for her daughter's treatment. She contacted several professionals who offered home-based services, interviewed two of these people, and settled on one. The consultant she selected had his master's degree in special education and had worked for several years in a center-based program for young children with autism. He was open and frank about his training and his experience. Their consultant seemed quite knowledgeable about applied behavior analysis and was very much at ease when he worked with the M's daughter. The Ms contacted several other families with whom he worked and got rave reviews about his competence. Mrs. M noted that before they had hired their current consultant, she and her husband had spoken with one prospective consultant who did not have very good credentials and did not seem to have a truly professional attitude toward her work. Alice M warned the Gs that while there were some very good people offering home services, some of them were not well trained and not very good at what they did.

The consultant hired by Alice M came to the family's home to do an initial workshop, where he taught Mr. and Mrs. M and their assistants the basics of applied behavior analysis and gave them a set of teaching programs to do until the next visit. He helped them set up a quiet space in a corner of the family room where their

teaching center would be located. He also emphasized that he would expect to talk to them by telephone at least once a week to help fine tune their programs.

Although the consultant made suggestions about how to find help, it was up to the family to recruit the tutors who would actually conduct the teaching sessions with their daughter. The Ms lived close to a community college, which turned out to be a very good source of helpers. They also found two young people in their church who wanted to volunteer their help. Eventually, they identified four people who were interested in psychology or education, who liked small children, and who wanted to learn the instructional methods to be used in the programs for their daughter.

The Ms and their consultant trained the students in how to use applied behavior analysis, and these tutors did much of the actual teaching. However, Mrs. M herself spent many hours a week teaching and Mr. M worked with his daughter on the weekends. It was a demanding schedule made more complex because the family had a son just two years older than their daughter with autism. Meeting the needs of both children was exhausting, and both parents worried that they might be neglecting their older boy. They were, however, very gratified with the progress their daughter had made. Mrs. M told Grace and Allan that after two months of instruction their little girl was much easier to manage, was starting to use a few words, and followed a long list of instructions.

Grace and Allan were impressed by the M family's experience and talked at length about the merits of adopting a home-based program of their own. However, it would have meant a radical change in their lives and they were concerned about the level of sacrifice involved. For example, using home services would mean that Grace would have to quit her job as an office manager. This loss of income might mean they might have to sell their home. They were also concerned about financing the home-based program itself. Their school district was not willing to pay for the home-based program because they had several center-based programs in their community offering high quality behavioral programs. Ultimately, Grace and Allan decided against the home-based program and selected one of the center-based programs recommended by their school district. In talking about this decision several years later, they emphasized that it was the single most difficult decision they had to make about Tad's education and the one that caused them the most personal turmoil.

What Setting Is Best for Your Family?

A fundamental choice facing every parent of a young child with autism is whether that child's education ought to be based within their own home or in a school or other treatment facility. Both home-based and center-based models of treatment are in widespread use, and advocates for both approaches report substantial benefits from their efforts. To date, there have been no good research studies comparing these two approaches. Consequently, parents will need to rely on their own good judgement in making this decision. For the G family the final decision was partially economic. They did not see how they could afford a home-based program on Allan's salary, and if Grace were to be home to supervise the program, she would have to leave her job. In addition, they were impressed by the quality of two of the programs they had seen in the community and knew that they had good alternatives for Tad. They wondered what they would have done if their community had not been able to offer them a good choice for their son.

Making Choices

There are a number of factors to consider in making the choice between a home-based and center-based program. This chapter first provides a brief description of each model and reviews some of the pros and cons of each approach. Table 4-1 summarizes some of these factors.

Table 4-1 | Factors to Consider in Home-Based versus Center-Based Programs

- The Time Demands on Parents
- Degree of Parental Control over the Child's Educational Program
- Access to Multidisciplinary Team
- Availability of Experienced Teaching Staff
- Time Spent by the Child in Travel
- Time Spent in Required Activities
- Influence of Visual and Auditory Distractions
- The Availability of Normally Developing Peers
- The Age Appropriate Nature of Being at Home
- Impact on Family Finances

Home-Based Treatment

The term "home-based" refers to a treatment program that occurs, at least initially, within the child's own home. A room of the house, perhaps the child's bedroom or a family recreation room, is selected as the work area. Ideally the room should be relatively distraction free, with attractive items such as toys or video games out of sight and out of reach except when the trainer wants to offer them to the child. Small tables, chairs, and instructional materials are conveniently located so that the child's tutors can have easy access to them.

In the home-based model, parents contract with a professional service provider to come to their home to oversee their child's educational program. Sometimes this professional is a consultant who only visits the family periodically, and other times the consultant may do a large portion of the instruction with the child, as well as oversee the curriculum and train other team members. When the professional consults on a periodic basis, the family will typically take the initiative to find other team members who actually run the programs developed by the consultant. These team members may be volunteers from the community or persons who are paid for their services. Regardless of the level of involvement of the consultant, the parents themselves are almost always part of the team who are responsible for the child's education.

Finding good tutors is a task in itself. Among the most helpful places to look are the psychology, speech, and special education departments of colleges and universities, and churches, synagogues, and other volunteer groups. College students tend to be very bright, idealistic, and hard working. Those are excellent qualities to look for in a tutor! You can call a college and ask them to post notices describing the job and you can place a help wanted ad in the campus paper. You can also ask your priest, rabbi, or minister how to recruit volunteers from your church or synagogue. Although volunteers will save you money, it is not easy to find enough to people to fill a child's schedule. In addition, paying people may make you more comfortable about making demands on them.

After a child with autism has made sufficient progress within the home, steps are taken to provide exposure to other children. This can be arranged through playgroups, summer day camps, other recreational groups, and nursery school or day care settings. Ultimately, if the treatment goes well, the child would be moved into a regular education setting such as kindergarten or first grade.

Center-Based Treatment

Center-based treatment usually occurs in a school, although it might be done in a classroom, in a hospital, or early intervention center. The same techniques of applied behavior analysis that are used in a home-based program can be used in a center-based one. Most center-based programs expect families to provide support for their work by carrying out some instructional programs in the home. However, the time demands on parents involved in center-based programs are more modest than for those involved in home-based programs. Children in center-based programs, like those in home-based programs, are usually systematically introduced to settings where they can interact with normally developing peers.

Both the home-based and the center-based programs have advantages and disadvantages. Taking these factors into account may help you make your own decision about which direction you prefer to go and which is realistic for your family.

The Pros and Cons

Demands on Parents

In a home-based model, parents have the primary responsibility for coordinating their child's education. They may be responsible for a significant portion of the child's direct instruction. Even if they have a full cadre of helpers to do most of the teaching, the parents typically coordinate everyone's efforts, train new team members, and ensure that everyone is working on the same tasks in the same fashion. Their home consultant provides them with instructional programs and ensures that the child is making good progress in a well-developed instructional sequence. The home consultant also trains the parents and the tutors in the teaching methods.

Because of the high degree of responsibility for their child's education, parents who use a home-based model must be highly skilled in the use of applied behavior analysis and able to make day-by-day decisions about their child's progress within programs. By contrast, in a center-based program, the child's teacher usually plays the role of coordinator and supervisor. The teacher, who typically has a degree in special education, and may also be certified in early childhood education, has back-up support from a team of professional consultants. Although parents play a crucial role in ensuring that material taught in a center-based model is transferred to the home and to the child's regular routine, this is far less daunting for most parents than being the person with primary instructional responsibility.

The home-based model works best in families where one parent can remain at home to oversee the child's progress. That usually rules out the use of this model in families where both parents must work to support the family. When one parent does stay home, it is most often mothers who oversee their child's program. However, we know several fathers who supervise their child's home program. Among the factors that parents take into account in deciding which parent will stay home are the personalities of the parents, their ability to tolerate the demands of the task, and the income-earning potential of each partner. For example, in one family we know the mother is a highly paid attorney and the father a more modestly compensated high school guidance counselor. They decided it would be easier to live on the mother's income and have the father stay home than vice versa. They also commented to us that the father was a slower-paced, more relaxed person who could adapt more readily to being

home full time than could the mother. Each family using a home-based program needs to consider these sorts of factors in deciding who will remain at home and who will work outside of the home.

Grandparents, aunts, uncles, and other family members may sometimes play a central role in the education of a child with autism. For example, they may act as one of the child's "tutors." Rarely, they may be the person who coordinates a child's instruction. However, because it is a time-consuming role that requires a great deal of control and decision-making about the child, asking a close family member or a good friend to assume this supervisory role may complicate the relationships in a family. Therefore, you should think carefully about how this arrangement would fit in your own circumstances.

Sometimes parents have little if any choice about assuming the primary instructional role for their child. For example, if you live in an isolated area where there are few resources, your only option may be to rely on home-based teaching. Your consultant may be someone who lives in a large city who flies in to see you on a regular basis. Similarly, if you live in a country where no one knows much about teaching children with autism, you have to take on a central role in your child's instruction because no one else knows how. Some families outside of the United States, Canada, and Western Europe rely on a home-based consultation model for their child.

For most single-parent families or for families in which both parents must work, the home-based model is not feasible. There also are some families who are facing multiple crises such as the illness of a grandparent, a parent, or another child. As a result of these circumstances they cannot devote the amount of time required for a home-based program. For these families, a center-based program is the sole option.

Parental Control Over the Child's Education

The concept of parental involvement is a sword that cuts two ways. Home-based programs require more parent involvement than do center-based, but they also give parents more complete control over their child's education. They are the people who call all the shots. Many of the parents who use a home-based approach are superbly skilled in applied behavior analysis. They also know their child's personality more intimately than could any professional. As a result, these parents are in an excellent position to make day-by-day and often minute-by-minute decisions about their child's progress on a particular instructional sequence. Because they love their child and are most deeply invested in her welfare, they may be ideal advocates and teachers for her.

In a center-based program, parents inevitably surrender some control to the professional staff. In a good program, when both parents and professionals are open to one another's ideas, that sharing can result in a smoothly running program in which there is a sense of common goals and mutual respect. Under these conditions, multiple partners can all contribute to the child's learning, and the family and child will benefit from that network of support. This collaborative approach does, however, place demands on all of the participants to learn to voice their opinions and concerns, listen carefully to one another, and be flexible in their approach.

Parents and professionals both share the burden of learning how to collaborate. Although it is part of the school personnel's job to listen with respect and care to parents, that listening and respect is a two-way street. Parents can support and encourage the teaching staff, and recognize that they too have their vulnerabilities and needs that may intrude on their objectivity. It is in the best interests of the child when all of the partners are willing to work at effective communication.

The Availability of a Multidisciplinary Team

In a center-based program there is typically a group of professionals available for consultation and service. Usually this group includes speech-language specialists, who have expertise in language development, and psychologists, who can consult in the creation of behavior management problems. Depending on your child's individual needs, other professionals, including physicians, physical therapists, and occupational therapists, may also be called on for consultation. When a child is in a home-based program, these additional services need to be sought out individually, and they might not be as easily coordinated as in a center-based program, where staff routinely talk with one another. That coordination among professionals becomes another task of the family.

The Use of Experienced Team Members

In an established center-based program there are a group of trained staff who are intimately familiar with the applied behavior analytic procedures that have been shown to be helpful in educating children with autism. These are usually full-time staff who are familiar with behavioral technology and have been extensively supervised in its application. Home-based programs often make use of non-professional tutors who must be trained before they are ready to work with the child. Even after training, these tutors need considerable on-going supervision.

Time Spent in Transportation

In a home-based program the staff comes to the child, while in a center-based program the child travels to the center. Time spent in travel is time not spent in instruction, and if a child has a long trip to the center, this can add up to a considerable part of the day. On the other hand, a number of parents have commented to us that their child naps on the bus on the way home, and arrives at the door full of new energy and ready to go. This issue of time spent in travel is a very individual one.

Time Spent in Required Activities

Center-based programs often have a number of required activities including nap time, lunch breaks, fire drills, and the like. These events may not be attuned to the needs of the individual child. On the other hand, these kinds of events are part of the normal routine of childhood and it is useful for a child to learn how to handle them. In a home-based program, breaks can be taken as the child needs them, and less total time is consumed when only one child needs to be taken to the toilet, fed lunch, and so forth.

The Influence of Visual and Auditory Distractions

Classrooms are often noisy places. Bring two or more children together in a small space and there will be noise. In a center-based program, children may be doing their one-to-one work in a small classroom where there are other adults and children working as well. The sounds and the sights of other people may be distracting to some young children with autism. One child's laughter or tantrum may distract another child's concentration. On the other hand, such distractions are part of the natural environment for every child, and the child with autism will have to learn to cope with the presence of others if she is to function in a more normalized setting. At the Douglass School, we reduce these distractions by working with each child in an individual cubby. In a home-based program, an environment can be created that is essentially distraction free. Eventually the child will have to be weaned from that level of quiet to a more normalized setting, but for some young children, beginning with a distraction-free setting can be helpful.

Ease of Access to Normally Developing Peers

Regardless of whether a child is in a home-based or a center-based program, it is important to provide contact with normally developing peers. In a center-based program, there is often a ready made procedure for creating this opportunity. The peers may be enrolled in the same school or even the same class, or there may be an arrangement with a nearby school to offer that integrated experience. Families using home-based programs often have to make their own arrangements to integrate their child with normally developing peers and then directly supervise that integration.

The Age of the Child

Many typically developing young children spend their entire day at home. Although less common than it was a couple of generations ago, it is still not unusual for the parent of a preschool-aged child to be home full-time with that child. The use of a home-based program in the early years is therefore consistent in some ways with the amount of time that a parent might give to a normally developing child. However, in our contemporary western society, children who are approaching school age typically have some sort of social experience beyond the home. We do not know of any data concerning the value of home-based instruction for children beyond the pre-school years. One could argue that in most cases it would be highly artificial to have an older child with autism isolated from her same-age peers.

The Impact on Family Finances

The cost of running a good home-based program can range between $20,000 and $40,000 a year in 1998 U.S. dollars. Of course, if you rely primarily on family and volunteers, it will cost less than if you hire several professionals to work with your child. Given that many families lack the personal funds and/or the time to do this work, it is typically the role of the school district to pay for the services.

Not every school district will agree readily to a home-based program. They are expensive to provide, and if there are several preschool-aged children with autism in a community, it may not be cost-effective to educate each child in his or her own home.

Some schools may resist home-based programs because they may not be the "least restrictive environment." It may help in these cases to remind the school personnel that very young children typically remain at home with their parents, and that home is the most "natural" environment for a small child. In addition, you could point out that the home setting does not have many of the visual and auditory distractions that can be a problem for children with autism in a school setting.

Some parents, committed to the value of the home-based model, have turned to litigation to pressure a school system to provide the funds to support a home-based program. Sometimes the family prevails in these legal proceedings and sometimes the school district prevails. There is no assurance that a lawsuit will result in obtaining a home-based program. Some affluent families may be able to pay the educational bill themselves, but home-based programs of the level of intensity and behavioral sophistication necessary to provide appropriate treatment are very expensive. Unless an outside agency pays the bill, it may be impossible for most families to have access to this service.

There are some strategies a family can use to try to persuade their school district to pay for a home-based program including the cost of tutors and consultants, or to create a center-based program within the district. One thing you can do is to help the district professionals become aware of the empirical support available for the use of applied behavior analysis. Pointing out the research studies and sharing books such as ours may help the members of the child study team become familiar with why this treatment is so vital. If you are already using these methods at home, you may also want to videotape sessions of your child being taught by the use of applied behavior analysis. You could tape one of the very first sessions when your child may have been resistant and difficult, and then a session a little later when she has become cooperative and responsive. If your child hasn't started using ABA yet, you might use the videotapes made by Ivar Lovaas and Ronald Leaf to illustrate the benefits of ABA treatment. Similarly, showing data on your child's mastery of new skills, or data from another child's program, if your child hasn't begun a program, would be a good way to document how she benefits from the teaching approach. You might also contrast your child's progress using applied behavior analysis with her progress in previous teaching attempts.

If you're interested in having your child participate in a program even though it's out of your school district, the staff at the program might be able to help you with arguments to persuade your school district to send your child there. They might also be willing to speak to officials from your school district about what's involved in setting up and maintaining such a program. Finally, have a consultant in applied behavior analysis come to the IEP or IFSP meeting to speak directly with the team members about the teaching methods.

Even if your district is adamant about not paying for your home program, they may still be willing to pay for related services such as speech and language therapy. Do take advantage of every opportunity they offer as long as the methods being used in these related services are compatible with your home-based program.

Finally, if data, logic, and the law all fail you in your efforts to establish the kind of center-based or home-based program your child requires, use every ounce of creativity to get the resources your child needs. Remember, the best gains are made by children who start a program of intensive behavioral intervention early. Do what you must to get this help. That can include setting up your own program, moving to another community where better services are available, recruiting volunteers, going to the newspaper with your story, and so forth.

In Sum

The choice between a home-based and center-based program is not always clear cut. A number of factors should be weighed in making a decision for your child. These include the quality of the center-based programs available in your community, the resources available for home-based instruction, and the needs of your family. At our own center, we offer both home-based and center-based services to ensure that families have a choice of services. Since there is no good data documenting that one model or the other is superior, the most important thing to evaluate is the competency of the professionals who offer the services. In center-based programs, you generally have some assurance of competency because staff are typically accountable to a supervisor. However, there are at present no credential requirements for home-based consultants, and anyone who wishes can claim to be an expert and offer his or her services. When it comes to home-based programs, that old adage "Let the buyer beware" is a sound warning. You owe it to your child to be a well-informed consumer.

Parents Speak

Running a home-based program can be very hard on the family life itself. Depending on how many hours per week you have therapy, it puts a strain financially and mentally on the family. Our lives revolved around his therapy schedule. I was also involved with hiring therapists, making up their schedules, and trying to rearrange sessions when they couldn't keep their appointment time. When I couldn't get someone to fill in I was so frustrated. He wasn't getting the therapy he so desperately needed and I wasn't getting the free time I so desperately needed. I also have a seven-year-old son who needs me too and I always have to arrange his schedule around his brother's.

Having the home-based program was working great. He was making tremendous progress and was changing into a different little boy. However, it was time for him to go to school. As much as I hate to admit it—we both needed a break from each other. I wanted him to go to a school that had the intensive program he had at home and I wanted him to start to develop social skills. If he was ever going to be mainstreamed some day, he would need those skills. Putting my baby on that bus at age three was the hardest thing I ever had to do. I cried so hard when he waved goodbye that first day. Fortunately, he loves going on the bus so it makes it much easier for me to let go.

∞

The home-based program was terrific. She made good progress and we always knew what was going on. But, it came at a big price. I had to quit my job and my husband ended up working overtime almost every night. We had to take out a second mortgage too. For more than year we hardly saw each other. When the weekends came we were both exhausted. This year she has been put in a regular first grade, but she still needs a lot of help. I'm not sure how this is going to work out. I do know that without the home-based program she might not have gone anywhere. We don't have any special autism programs in our community and I really needed the help I got. Our therapists were great.

∞

Most of the people who have helped our son have been wonderful. But in the beginning we interviewed someone who was *a loser. She told us she could set up a complete program for our son, train our tutors and us, and develop the curriculum. When we checked her references, we found out her only training was six months as an assistant in a classroom. Parents need to be careful who they hire.*

⟲

I knew from the beginning that we wanted Tim in a school. My husband I both work and we couldn't stop. I guess we're lucky because there are great schools in our state and we got Tim into one that uses applied behavior analysis. Plus, the school district was great. They worked with us every step of the way. The school psychologists told us they know that if Tim gets a good start now it will be best for him and probably save the taxpayers thousands of dollars too.

⟲

Home programming is essential. Autistic children won't succeed if they get mixed messages. What's done at school must also be done at home.

⟲

We have begun scaling back on his home therapy and filling the time with organized activities. In particular, two months ago we enrolled him in karate school. The instructors were not told that he had a problem and so far no one has asked.

References

The Lovaas Learning Tapes can be ordered from Pro-Ed. Their address is 8700 Shoal Creek Blvd., Austin, TX 78757-6897. 800-397-7633.

5 | What to Teach and How to Teach It: Curriculum and Teaching Programs

The G Family Learns about Programming

During a tour of an intensive behavioral preschool, Grace and Allan had the opportunity to look at the instructional materials used by that center. There was a multi-page listing of the many potential goals a teacher might select for students in her class, and a series of notebooks crammed full of specific programs with details about how to teach the skills listed on the master curriculum. The program sheets looked confusing at first glance, but it became evident that they reflected a vital component of the center's expertise. Each sheet provided a systematic description of how to teach a particular skill. The director told the Gs that the teachers drew on these materials in setting up each child's instructional plans, but it was often necessary to modify the programs to meet the needs of an individual child. It was not just a matter of turning to the right page and following the directions in a cookbook fashion. Frequently the teacher had to try a program, modify it according to a child's response, and try again.

The program sheets included a number of technical terms such as "Sd," "prompt," and "reinforcement," which Grace and Allan knew were the jargon of applied behavior analysis. The director assured them that part of the training process for new parents was helping them understand this terminology so that they could support and be part of the learning that went on in the school. The words might sound technical, but they were not in fact so mysterious, and it would not take long to understand this vocabulary well enough to read a sheet and implement a program.

What Does the G Family's Experience Mean for You?

A quality program for the education of children with autism will have a complete curriculum to draw upon for instructional purposes. This curriculum is the road map that guides teachers in moving from one goal to the next. The curriculum must be flexible, and the specific programs being used must be modified according to a child's *learning style*—that is, according to the ways he processes information best. Some children may benefit more from visual input, others from auditory input or from using a

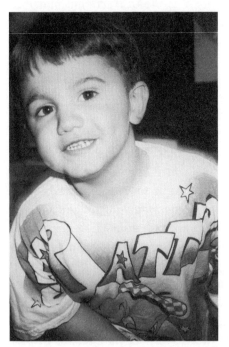

motor skill such as tracing letters with a finger while naming them. Because there are so many individual differences among children, it is important that the curriculum be adaptable to the style of every child.

Grace and Allan may have been a bit intimidated by the technical vocabulary they saw on the program sheets, but most parents are able to master this terminology without too much difficulty. Once you know the basics of behavioral language, you will be able to read and understand many of the instructional materials used in any teaching program. However, the behavioral skills involved in actually implementing these procedures require supervised experience to do well. Both parents and teachers alike should be well trained before they undertake this highly sophisticated instruction. That training must included hands-on supervised work.

Although the specific details of a curriculum will vary somewhat from one center to another, the broad outlines will doubtless look similar. There will be programs to teach a child to follow instructions, to imitate what an adult or another child does, to use speech in functional ways, to play with toys, to play with another person, and so forth. Most preschool curricula respect the developmental nature of how children learn, and arrange these skills in a sequence that respects how one skill builds on another. For example, a child will be asked to imitate sounds before imitating words, or to match identical items before recognizing ones that are different. Some centers have a better-developed and more nuanced curriculum than others. This variation in quality is especially likely to be apparent when it comes to teaching advanced skills for language and socialization. It requires a great deal of know-how to create effective teaching programs for these skills.

Centers also vary in the specific strategies that are used to teach a skill. In centers where staff is more sophisticated in the use of applied behavior analysis, teachers are likely to apply behavioral methods with greater elegance than in centers where staff has only a passing familiarity with this technology. However, even very good teachers will differ in some of their teaching methods because not every aspect of applied behavior analysis has been objectively studied. For example, some teachers use "behavior specific praise" and some do not. That is, some teachers will name the behavior just completed by the child (e.g., "Good clapping"), while others will use more general praise (e.g., "Great work").

In this chapter, we will move from discussing the broad details of curriculum to describing the specific details of one little boy's instructional programs. Although there will not be enough detail to equip you to create programs for your child, this material will help you understand what goes into creating a curriculum.

A Sample Preschool Curriculum

The material in this chapter is based on the curriculum used at the Douglass School, our on-campus school for children with autism at Rutgers, the State University of New Jersey. For more than 25 years, the Douglass School staff have been refining and developing this instructional material. Countless teachers and supervisors have contributed to its development and the material is part of a shared pool of information. It is not possible to give credit to any one person for a specific program because we have built one upon the other for a quarter century. The samples in this chapter reflect our collective creative effort. Similar work has been going on in other centers, and some of our teaching programs are undoubtedly similar to those in other programs around the nation. This similarity arises because: 1) there are a number of tasks that are recognized as essential for children to learn; and 2) because behavioral teaching strategies are used in similar ways. In addition, many former staff members from Douglass School have gone to work at other places and taken parts of the curriculum with them when they went. Like the legendary Johnny Appleseed walking through America sowing apple trees, that process has spread some of our curriculum items far and wide!

A good curriculum should be a highly detailed itinerary describing the many, many skills that need to be mastered by a child during the process of growing up. These skills should be organized in a logical fashion, and broken into small enough units that the child does not have to take any "giant steps" from one item to the next. However, even the best curriculum has its limits. One of the things a curriculum does not tell us is how long it will take a child to learn a skill. Nor does a good curriculum ensure that a child will, in fact, learn all of the skills we would like him to master. Some children will progress slowly from item to item and may not be able to master every goal. Other children will move rapidly through instructional programs and at times will take leaps that allow them to move quickly from basic material to more advanced tasks. A child's progress may also be uneven from area to area. He may do quite well with gross motor skills and have more difficulties with language or socialization tasks. It is therefore important that each child be provided with an individualized instructional program that matches his own pace.

As the first step in developing an individualized program, the teacher will begin by assessing the child's current skills in each of the general areas on the curriculum. For example, she will explore the child's abilities in expressive and receptive language, social skills, and self-help activities. She will present tasks from various levels in each category and observe how the child performs on them. This checklist of skills is maintained over the years to show how the child has progressed.

Many parents express concern about the "level" of programming at the beginning of intervention. It is not uncommon to feel that the first programs being taught involve skills your child can already demonstrate. These foundation skills, however, are critically important. It is essential that the child *consistently* demonstrate these skills. It is not enough for the child to demonstrate a behavior "when he feels like it," or only occasionally. We need to be able to rely on these behaviors in order to build more complex skills.

It is not feasible to include here all of the instructional material from any domain of the curriculum we use at the Douglass School. What follows are samples to give you a sense of how this material is organized. It would take a book or two to describe all of the many programs that comprise the total curriculum.

The Organization of a Curriculum

The components of a curriculum can be broken into broad categories including gross motor, fine motor, expressive language, receptive language, self-help, social skills, and academic/cognitive skills (Table 5-1). As shown in Table 5-2, these general categories can themselves be subdivided into finer units. For example, under the heading of gross motor skills are such specific skills as stair climbing and running, as well as more advanced skills for playing a ball game. Self-help skills progress from the basics of feeding, dressing, and washing to more complex ones such as simple meal preparation, taking a shower, and selecting clothing for the day.

Table 5-1 | Some Broad Areas of the Douglass School Curriculum

- ◆ Pre-Academic and Academic
- ◆ Expressive Language
- ◆ Receptive Language
- ◆ Concept Formation
- ◆ Fine Motor
- ◆ Gross Motor
- ◆ Self-Help
- ◆ Socialization and Play
- ◆ Maladaptive Behavior

Table 5-2 | Examples of Sub-Headings under Gross Motor Skills

- Stair climbing
- Running
- Jumping/hopping
- Balance/coordination

Compliance Training

Compliance is a major issue for most children with autism. Many children respond to nearly any adult request with instantaneous resistance and attempts to escape from the demand. Most children with autism need to build a capacity for tolerance of teacher-led activities. This can be done with systematic teaching procedures.

It is often difficult for parents to recognize the necessity of compliance training. In fact, it can be painful to subject your child to demands, particularly if his resistance is intense. A child's tears, tantrums, or aggression are frequently enough to deter a parent from following through with a request. In addition, parents often worry that their child is "bored" with many repetitions of a task. Almost universally, parents of children with autism will report that their children "sometimes" demonstrate a particular skill. They may say that "she will do it when she is in the mood."

This lack of consistency in a child's response to adult instructions is a reflection of problems in focusing attention and compliance difficulties commonly seem in autism. It is necessary to build consistency in the child's ability to demonstrate skills. This is the only way to ensure that the foundation skills are truly established.

For a child for whom noncompliance is a frequent and intense response, we begin by teaching him to tolerate the teaching context itself. Sitting in a chair on request is a significant challenge for some children and may have to be taught before any other target skills. The instructor may simply increase the amount of time the child spends in the chair. First it may be 1 second, then 2 seconds, 3 seconds, 5 seconds, and so forth. Favorite toys may be made available to the child in the chair to increase the reinforcing power of sitting there. Gradually, other instructional demands will be paired with sitting.

Parents sometimes ask, "Does he really need to sit in a chair?" The reason that a particular work location and chair are chosen is to help the child discriminate "work" from "play." He learns that demands will be made when he sits in the chair, but not when he takes a break and sits on the floor. Ultimately, most children are helped by the use of clear cues to recognize and respond to the instructional setting. Of course, the details of shaping your child's tolerance for work will be individually determined. Some very young children, for example, sit on the floor to work. The professional guiding your program will help you develop a program that is right for your child.

Imitation

One of the most salient deficits of children with autism is their lack of imitative skills. They do not watch and do what those around them are doing. This deficit may be an early reflection of the same problems that result in difficulties with play and social skills. It is therefore critical for early intervention treatment plans to place a primary emphasis on imitation.

Teaching children to watch others and do as they do helps them learn to use objects and toys for functional purposes, to imitate facial movements needed to make certain sounds, and to follow along with a group. Both imitating motor movements such as stamping feet or touching the head, and imitating use of objects such as stacking blocks or rolling a car, need to be taught specially and systematically. Sample hierarchies for teaching in these areas are listed in Table 5-3. Instructions begin with very concrete one-step actions such as touching one's head or clapping. Because the focus is on imitation, the instruction to imitate clapping would not be "Clap your hands." Rather, the adult would say "Do this" and clap her hands. As skills in simple imitation

Table 5-3 | Imitation Skills

General Progression of Motor Imitation

One-Step Commands
  A. Gross motor in chair (e.g., clap, arms up, stamp feet)
  B. Gross motor out of chair (e.g., jump, turn around)
  C. Fine motor (e.g., make a fist, point, thumbs up)
  D. Facial (e.g., stick out tongue, blow kiss)

Two-Step Commands
  A. Related (e.g., stand up and jump)
  B. Unrelated (e.g., clap and touch nose)

Three-Step Commands

Peer Imitation (imitating a child rather than an adult)

Generalization/Extensions of Imitation
  Actions to songs (e.g., "The Wheels on the Bus")
  Obstacle course (e.g., climbing over, around & under obstacles
    with another child)
  Observational learning (learning in group from other children)
  Imitation games (e.g., "Simon Says")

General Progression of Imitation of Object Manipulation

One-Step Imitation
  A. Simple discrete actions (e.g., block in bucket, ring on stacker)
  B. Complex discrete actions (e.g., roll car on table, put bottle to
    baby's mouth)

Two-Step Imitation
  A. Related (e.g., put man in car & roll car, put baby in cradle
    & rock)
  B. Unrelated (e.g., put block in bucket & ring on stacker, put
    man in car & peg in pegboard)

Three-Step Imitation
  Related sequence at theme-based activity centers (e.g., farm
  toy, dollhouse, or amusement park toy)

Generalizations/Extensions of Imitation
  Pretend play with props (e.g., dress-up clothing, play kitchen)
  Task completion (finishing activity with toy)
  Peer imitation (playing with toys as peers do)
  Observational learning (learning to use toys or play games by
    watching peers)

Table 5-4 | Some Skills Required for Stair Climbing

1. Walks up stairs two feet per stair when held by one hand
   15-17 months

2. Walks down stairs two feet per stair when held by one hand
   15-17 months

3. Walks up stairs, alternating feet, using railing
   32-36 months

4. Walks independently up stairs, alternating feet
   36-48 months

5. Descends stairs by alternating feet, holding rail
   36-48 months

6. Independently descends stairs, alternating feet
   48-60 months

7. Walks up stairs, holding objects in both hands
   60-72 months

8. Walks down stairs, holding objects in both hands
   60-72 months

---

develop, two- and three-step imitation is taught. For example, in a three-step command, the child might watch as an adult claps her hands, puts a block in a box, and folds her hands on the table. It is important to remember that the specific actions are not as important as the process of learning to watch and follow what other people do.

Gross Motor Skills

The term "gross motor skills" refers to the use of large muscle groups such as those involved in jumping, running, and climbing. This term can be distinguished from "fine motor skills," which refers to more detailed precise muscle movements such as those required to pick up a peg or hold a pencil.

Each gross motor skill on a child's curriculum, such as stair climbing, is broken down into its multiple component parts (See

Table 5-4). To break stair climbing into its components, you could teach a child first to walk upstairs with one hand held, then to walk down with one hand held. Next the child would learn to walk up while holding a railing, and so forth. To help our teachers identify age-appropriate goals for motor skills, where physical maturation is crucial, we often include the average age at which normally developing children would master a target skill. However, age alone is not a sufficient determinant of a goal and for the child with autism sequencing is based on the child's strengths and special needs rather than primarily on age. A child may be at or above age level in one domain and far below in another. Each goal is selected in light of the child's current abilities, not just his age.

Speech and Language

Receptive language refers to the ability to decode another person's communication, while expressive language refers to the ability to communicate using speech or an alternative mode of communication such as use of a language board. Receptive and expressive language are a vital part of the instructional program

---

Table 5-5 | Sample Receptive Language Skills in the Douglass School Curriculum

- Points to desired object
- Follows one-step command to "give"
- Points to five body parts on self
- Discriminates actions in pictures
- Demonstrates functional use of objects
- Points to self in a group photo
- Knows concept of big and little using pictures
- Demonstrates comprehension of preposition "on" in relation to self
- Demonstrates comprehension of preposition "over" in relation to pictures

Table 5-6 | Sample Expressive Language Skills in the Douglass School Curriculum

- Verbalizes "no"
- Answers "what" questions regarding picture
- Answers "where" questions regarding here and now
- Names 3 pictures of actions
- Asks simple questions ("what's that?")
- Names most body parts
- Names own age

of every young child with autism. The Douglass School curriculum has a detailed sequence of items in these domains. The receptive sequence begins with very basic skills such as "turns head when name is called" and "points to desired object," progresses to "following one-step commands" and "demonstrating functional use of objects," and moves to more advanced skills such as "understanding opposites" and "recognizing same and different." Table 5-5 includes a sampling of items from various levels of this receptive language curriculum. The specific beginning point on this list for any child is determined by his performance on the teacher's pre-assessment. In Table 5-6, a parallel set of goals for expressive language is listed. Again, these begin with early skills such as babbling for a child who makes no sounds, progress to verbal imitation, which is a crucial skill, and advance to naming objects, naming actions, and answering the "Wh" questions (who, what, when, why). The ability to imitate is a key precursor to the development of expressive language.

Social and Play Skills

Like language skills, social skills are an essential part of the curriculum for every child with autism. The Douglass School curriculum is very detailed in this domain. (See Table 5-7.) Early

---

Table 5-7 | Sample Social Skills from the Douglass School Curriculum

- Responds to direction "look at me"
- Responds to adult praise, rewards, promises
- Engages in parallel play
- Identifies other children by gender
- Joins in finger plays and action songs
- Helps with household chores
- Performs for others
- Engages in role play/pretend play

---

social skills include such behaviors as looking at oneself in the mirror and playing peek-a-boo. This basic awareness of self and others then branches out into skills for solo play, play with an adult, play with a child, and play in a group. It also includes learning the many social behaviors important to school life such as sitting in a circle, following group directions, and learning to assert oneself in an appropriate fashion.

Maladaptive Behavior

Every curriculum for preschool children with autism needs to include ways to handle maladaptive behavior such as temper tantrums, aggression, or noncompliance. Not surprisingly, having autism can be very frustrating to children. They cannot easily learn the skills that give other children a sense of control over their environment. For example, a child may not be able to say "no" to an unwanted demand, and may therefore resort to tantrums instead. Children with autism may also exhibit maladaptive behavior because they enjoy making body movements that other children do not typically find pleasurable. For example, a child with autism may flap his fingers or stare at his hands. It is important to help the child gain control over these maladaptive or interfering behaviors

Table 5-8 | Sample Curriculum Items Related to Maladaptive Behavior

Aggression
- Decrease hitting
- Decrease kicking
- Decrease scratching
- Decrease head butting
- Decrease pushing

Stereotypic or Self-stimulatory Behavior
- Decrease rocking
- Decrease hand waving/finger play
- Decrease spinning
- Decrease head weaving

by learning more adaptive ways of coping with demands and more appropriate ways of obtaining pleasure.

Curriculum goals in the area of maladaptive behavior do not lend themselves to a developmental or age-appropriate hierarchy in the same way that speech or fine motor skills do. Rather, at the Douglass School this section of the curriculum consists of an extended list of maladaptive behaviors grouped according to target or possible function. (See Table 5-8.) For example, one broad category includes self-directed aggression and another relates to aggression toward others. There are categories for stereotypic or self-stimulatory behaviors, for noncompliance, and for eating problems.

Before any intervention is used to reduce the frequency of a child's inappropriate behavior we must do an assessment to attempt to understand the function of the behavior. For example, is the child tantruming to gain attention or to avoid work? Once that function is understood the teacher may draw from several different procedures in the curriculum. Most programs treat the problem behavior by teaching the child a substitute for the unwanted or inappropriate behavior. When the maladaptive behavior is especially troublesome, one of the psychologists on our staff is available to consult with the teacher about doing a special assessment and tailoring the intervention to the child's needs.

Instructional Programs

A curriculum that consisted solely of a well-developed list of instructional goals would be of some help in developing an educational plan for a child with autism. However, in order to be truly useful, these lists must be linked to specific teaching programs. An effective curriculum should not only suggest a sequence of skills, but also tell the teacher how to teach those skills. For example, if your child has learned how to answer "who" questions and is ready to move on to "what," there should be a program describing how to accomplish the new goals. These detailed instructional programs are at the heart of a child's education.

Understanding the Program Form

At the Douglass School we use a special form for each instructional program (see Figure 5-1). This Program Form provides a standardized format, ensuring that all the information is provided in a consistent fashion. If you can understand one Program Form, you will be able to read others as well. Table 5-9 lists the technical terms used on this form and gives a brief definition of each.

Figure 5-2 depicts an actual instructional program used for Charlie, a child at the Douglass School. This particular instructional program is from Charlie's first year in our school while he was still receiving primarily one-to-one instruction. Charlie was having problems making some sounds and needed help in learning how to place his tongue and lips to better articulate these sounds. This program, from the speech portion of the curriculum, was intended to help Charlie learn to imitate facial expressions.

There is a great deal of information included on the Program Form if you know how to read it. As you look at Figure 5-2,

Table 5-9 | Program Form Terminology

Behavioral Objective: Defines in observable terms the behavior under study. For example, the goal of reducing noncompliance might be defined as "John will comply with any instruction within 3 to 5 seconds of the command."

Behavior Specific Praise: Rather than just saying "Good boy," it is often helpful to tell a child exactly what he did right. An example of behavior specific praise would be, "I like the way you put your toys away."

Consequence: A consequence is what happens as a result of the child's responding or failing to respond to an instruction. One common consequence of a correct response is to reinforce (reward) the child. If a child fails to respond or makes a mistake, the consequence may be a *prompt* to guide a correct response.

Criterion: We need to decide when we will agree that a child has mastered a skill. Typically this calls for between 80% and 90% correct performance over two days. However, the criterion can be set at any level.

Data: Decision making in applied behavior analysis depends on the child's performance on a task. In order to evaluate progress we collect data. That is, we make a record of how often the child is correct and how often he makes mistakes.

Probe: A probe is a procedure used to collect a sample of a child's progress in a teaching program. For example, a teacher might collect "probe data" by recording a child's correct and incorrect responses for the last 10 trials of every teaching session.

Prompt: A visual, verbal, or motor gesture that cues a child about what to do. This can range from a full prompt such as "Say 'duck'" to a partial prompt such as "d...." Prompts are gradually faded as the child becomes more independent.

Sd: An Sd is a verbal instruction or other signal to a child that it is time to engage in a behavior. Examples of an Sd would be "do this" or "point to cow." If we teach a child to come to his mother when she blows a whistle, the sound of the whistle would be an Sd.

Target Behavior: A target behavior is the behavior being taught. Examples of target behaviors would be shoe tying, hand washing, or pointing to objects when named.

Figure 5-1

DOUGLASS SCHOOL

Educational Program Form

Student: School Year:

Area: Coordinator:

                                  Date Initiated:

                                  Date Mastered:

Target Behavior:

Behavioral Objective:

Description of Program:

Sd for Target Behavior:

Consequence:

Procedure:

Prompt Hierarchy:

Generalization:

Sets:

Materials:

Data:

Trials:

Criterion:

Program Comments:

notice that there is a brief description of the *Target Behavior* that is described as "Imitates facial expressions: Oral motor movements." This target is then translated into the *Behavioral Objective* of imitating ". . . oral motor movements within 3-5 seconds of the Sd [Discriminative Stimulus] presentation."

The abbreviation Sd (pronounced S D) is used in a Program Form to refer to an instruction or other event that tells a child it is time to do something. An example of an Sd would be "Give me the book" or "Point to blue." An Sd can sometimes be nonverbal. For example, we might teach a child to wave when he sees another person wave. In that case the Sd would be the waving gesture of another person. In Charlie's program as shown in Figure 5-2 the Sd is both auditory ("Do this") and visual (the action is performed). That instruction is the signal to Charlie to respond by copying his teacher's behavior. Prior to being taught the relatively complex oral motor behaviors used in this program, Charlie had learned to imitate an adult on the command of "Do this" for simple behaviors such as clapping his hands or stamping his feet. Incidentally, there are many kinds of stimuli in applied behavior analysis (e.g., reinforcing and discriminative) and the *type* of stimulus is always shown by the second letter. For example, the symbol for a reinforcing stimulus is Sr.

In Charlie's program under the heading of *Description of Program,* the teacher is called upon to be certain she has Charlie's attention and that he is sitting quietly before she starts her instruction. However, not every applied behavior analyst requires these attending skills from the child before giving the instructions. Rather, they assume that as the child learns that following instructions brings rewards for responding correctly, the child will learn to attend and will not become dependent on an adult's instructions to do so. This is a good example of an area in which experts differ. In practice, it is important to determine which approach is better for your child.

The learning we are asking Charlie to attempt is very demanding. We need to reward his efforts to help him stick to the task. Every instructional program therefore has a specified set of

Consequences. In this case, the teacher is told to reinforce Charlie with "behavior specific praise." Behavior specific praise means praise that identifies what he has done correctly. If Charlie sticks out his tongue just like his teacher in response to the command "do this," his teacher might say, "Good doing this." She might then give him a sip of soda or make a silly face that Charlie finds amusing. In that way she has praised his response, labeled what Charlie did correctly, and then used that very behavior as an opportunity for a playful interaction.

Not every teaching program uses behavior specific praise. In some programs the teacher simply praises the child without naming the target behavior. For example, she might say, "Great work." The reason for omitting behavior specific praise is that some children get confused by having the behavior labeled and believe they are being asked to repeat the target behavior. For example, if the teacher said, "Stamp your feet" and the child complied, the behavior specific praise of "Good stamping your feet" might be interpreted by the child as a command (Sd) to stamp his feet again.

Returning to our discussion of Charlie, if he does not respond to the Sd or makes a mistake, the teacher has been instructed to "prompt" a correct response. In the early stages of learning, she would physically manipulate his face to help him shape his mouth or hold out an item like a lollipop to encourage him to stick out his tongue. Later, she might use a subtler partial prompt such as tapping his lip very gently.

Another approach that the teacher might have taken if Charlie made an error is called the "No-No-Prompt" technique. In this method, once a child has shown that he is capable of making a correct response, the teacher says "No" in a neutral tone if the child makes an error. She then repeats the Sd. If he again makes an error she repeats "No." However, on the third trial she immediately prompts a correct response without giving the child an opportunity to make an error. Because some children may respond better to a correction after every error and some children may do better with the no-no-prompt method it is important to determine which works best for your child.

Figure 5-2

DOUGLASS SCHOOL

Educational Program Form

Student: Charlie Y   **School Year:** 95-96

Area: Speech   **Coordinator:** Sally/Rae

Date Initiated: 2/11/95   **Date Mastered:** 8/3/95

Target Behavior: Imitates facial expressions: oral motor
movements

Behavioral Objective: Charlie will imitate oral motor movements following a model within 3-5 seconds of Sd presentation

Description of Program: Establish sitting and attending
behavior

Sd for Target Behavior: "Do this"

Consequence: Reinforce correct responses with behavior
specific praise. If Charlie does not respond or responds
incorrectly, provide appropriate prompt. Implement correction
procedure and reinforce response with behavior specific praise.

Procedure:

Step 1: In a mirror side by side where Charlie can see your face
and his own, present Sd. Physically prompt him through the
movement using physical manipulation. Repeat the Sd.
Charlie is prompted to repeat the action.

Step 2: In a mirror side by side where Charlie can see your face
and his own, perform movement. Present Sd. Charlie is to
imitate the action.

Step 3: Siting face to face with Charlie, perform the movement.
Present Sd. Charlie is to independently imitate without
presence of the mirror.

Prompt Hierarchy:

1. Full Physical Prompt (e.g., lightly press lips together)
2. Partial Physical Prompt (e.g., lightly tap upper lip)
3. Partial Visual Prompt (e.g., point to Charlie's lip)

Generalization: Mastery requires that you probe this skill
varying the Sd, using at least two novel settings, sets of

Figure 5-2 continued

materials, and people. Criterion — 80% or above on at least three different days.

Sets:
1. lips together
2. open mouth
3. review Sets 1 & 2 mixed (Step 3 only)
4. kissing
5. bites lower lip
6. review sets 4 & 5 mixed (Step 3 only)
7. Places tongue between teeth

Materials: Mirror

Data: + = correct response, - = incorrect response, p = prompted response

Trials: 10 to 20 trials

Criterion: 90% correct over two sessions

Program Comments:
1. Use food as needed
2. As Charlie masters each set in this program, related sets can be introduced in the imitation of words/syllables program. For example, mastery of Set 1 (lips together) would indicate introduction of words such as "me, bee, pie."

The next section of the program sheet describes the specific teaching *Procedure* in successive steps. In Step 1 the teacher or speech-language therapist sits next to the child and both face a mirror. First she gives the Sd "do this" and immediately she physically prompts Charlie to imitate. Then she repeats the command "do this," shows the model, but does not prompt and waits for Charlie to respond. She only prompts him if he does not comply after 5 seconds. In Step 2 the prompts are not routinely offered at the start of each trial and are reserved for trials in which Charlie does not obey the command. Finally, in Step 3 the mirror is removed and Charlie must respond when facing the therapist.

The *Prompt Hierarchy* describes the kinds of prompts to be used and the order of the prompts. For example, the speech-language therapist is told to initially use a full prompt in which she helps Charlie press his lips together. Later she is to tap his lip, and

Table 5-10 | Speech and Language Programs Mastered by Charlie in One Year

- Follows commands with two objects (e.g., put the block and the cup on the table)
- Names object based on verbal information
- Uses subject pronouns (I, you, he, she, and it)
- Correctly responds to what questions: Describes use of senses
- Correctly responds to "when" questions
- Discriminates among who, what, where questions
- Labels shapes (rectangle, oval, and diamond)
- Understands and uses prepositions
- Labels texture of object
- Uses adjective-noun combinations appropriately
- Names sensations
- Answers specific questions about activity just completed
- Uses irregular past tense

eventually, if necessary, to point to his lip. Because children with autism can become quite dependent on prompts, this guidance is always to be decreased in intensity as quickly as possible and used no more than essential.

Children with autism have problems transferring (generalizing) their skills from one setting to the next. As a result it is important to plan for *Generalization* when writing their teaching programs. For example, Charlie must learn to imitate not only the specific behaviors that are being taught in the program, but new ones as well. We might test for this kind of generalization by modeling putting our tongue on our upper lip (a behavior he has not been taught) and seeing if he could imitate that new behavior. If he did, we would have evidence that he was able to generalize his responses to new but similar behaviors. If he did not, we would teach more behaviors and then test again for generalization.

Generalization should also extend to other teachers and other settings. For example, in order to demonstrate generalization across people in imitating oral motor movements, Charlie would be expected to imitate his teacher and his mother as well as the speech-language therapist who initially trained him. For generalization to new places he would be expected to follow the direction "do this" when it was given at home as well as at school. Notice that according to the Program Form we have applied an 80% correct criterion to Charlie's performance in the generalization portion of the program. He must get 8 out of 10 trials correct for three days in a row on the generalization tasks before he advances to a new goal.

Another important form of generalization is across instructions. That is, a child should learn to follow different commands that mean the same thing (e.g., "Follow me," "Do this," "Copy me," and "Do what I do"). These instructions are all variations on the same theme and a child may encounter different wordings in the natural environment.

The *Sets* section of the program lists the specific skills Charlie is to master. This includes pressing his lips together, opening his

---

Table 5-11 | Some of the Social and Play Skills Mastered by Charlie in One Year

- Initiates social contact (e.g., asks another child, "Can I play with you?")
- Plays in a group of other children
- Cooperates in simple games with adult or child
- Interacts reciprocally in a group of children
- Assumes a character role (e.g., police officer, teacher, daddy)
- Acts out a familiar routine (e.g., going shopping)
- Reacts and interacts with a second child in make-believe scene
- Invites another child to play a specific game
- Chooses the correct emotional response for a given situation

mouth, and so forth. Notice that the first few items are ones that are most easily prompted with physical guidance while the later items, such as placing tongue between teeth, are harder to prompt. We expect that as Charlie learns to imitate oral movements he will need fewer and fewer prompts for each new movement. Notice also that Charlie is being taught to discriminate among the different items by mixing two or more items, one of which he already knows, in the same session. He must put his lips together when that is the model and open his mouth when that task is requested. In order to do this, Charlie must learn to attend carefully to the teacher's behavior.

In this particular program we did not specify any particular *Materials* except the mirror. For some programs, we might list items to be used in teaching, such as blocks, trucks, dolls, and so forth. In the *Data* section the therapist has been asked to record Charlie's performance using a "+" to signify that he was correct and a "-" when he was incorrect. Sometimes she might also be told to record a "p" to indicate he was prompted on a trial. At the bottom of the Program Form under *Trials* is information indicating that the therapist should do 10 to 20 trials a day, and that according to the *Criterion* section Charlie must respond at 90 percent correct over two sessions in a row before he moves to the next set of tasks. Finally, under *Program Comments* the speech therapist is told that she should use food as necessary to motivate Charlie and that as he masters the oral motor skills they should be incorporated into his other speech programs.

Programs Mastered Over One Year

Charlie worked on many instructional programs related to speech and language over the course of one year. Table 5-10 shows a partial list of speech and language programs he mastered during the year.

Along with his instruction in speech and language, Charlie also benefited from similarly detailed programs in the domains of social skills. See Table 5-11 for a list of the social and play programs he learned in a year. Inspecting the sample programs for social skills in Figures 5-3 and 5-4 may give you an idea of the complexity of creating a full curriculum for a child with autism. Even if the teacher works in a setting that has a fully developed curriculum, she must be able to select those programs that are suitable for a child and adapt them to the specific learning style of the child.

Although some of the early programming for items like noun labels or pointing to a color may seem relatively straightforward, the demands on teacher and child grow increasingly more complex. A good example of a more complex social skill is complimenting another child. Among the precursors to learning when and how to say nice things to someone else are: a) social initiations, b) adequate speech, c) understanding the context for giving others compliments, d) reciprocal conversation, e) respecting physical space, and so forth. Each of these skills in turn has its own precursors! It is this complexity which makes a skilled teacher or consultant so vital.

A Few Thorny Questions

Many parents share the same questions about applied behavior analysis when they are thinking about intensive behavioral intervention for their child. This section answers some questions that come up quite frequently.

Why Are Reinforcements Important?

The role of reinforcement is to increase the likelihood that a child will repeat a desired response. The verbal feedback that accompanies a tangible reward is another way of informing the child that he or she has made the correct response. Without that feedback, learning would be nearly impossible.

Because children with autism may not care about pleasing us and the learning required of them is so demanding, it is important to offer them rewards that are highly desirable. Although

Figure 5-3

DOUGLASS SCHOOL

Educational Program Form

Student: Charlie Y   **School Year:** 96-97

Area: Social Skills   **Coordinator:** Bob

Date Initiated: 10/2/96   **Date Mastered:** 12/11/96

Target Behavior: Keeping appropriate distance from other child
Behavioral Objective: Charlie will select a bubble to stand in
that is an appropriate distance from a peer. He will stand in
space while speaking to peer.
Description of Program: Establish group attention
Sd for Target Behavior: "Show me where you stand when you
talk to a friend"
Consequence: Each child will receive a chip for standing in the
circle the whole time
Procedure:
1. Discuss rules for standing near a friend
2. Select one child to stand in a circle
3. Select another child to pick the circle they would stand in if
they wanted to talk to that friend.
4. Once in the appropriate circle, the second child expresses the
rules: I'm not too close, I'm not too far, if I could reach my
arms out straight, I'd touch my friend's shoulders.
5. After saying the rules, the children say "hi" to each other
6. Second child receives a chip for doing 3-6
Prompt Hierarchy: Initially Charlie should not be in first three
couplets. Gradually move him forward until he goes first.
Whisper rules as needed.
Generalization: Ensure that Charlie can play game with every
other child in class.
Sets: Not applicable.
Materials: Bubble markers on floor.
Data: + = correct, - = incorrect, p = prompted. Collect as
probe data.

Figure 5-3 continued

> **Trials:** Charlie should have at least three turns each time game is played.
> **Criterion:** Selects correct bubble and repeats rules independently when playing game two days in succession.
> **Program Comments:** Entire preschool class plays game.

reinforcements (rewards) can include tangible things like food, tickles, and hugs, good teachers always combine these items with verbal praise. When words of approval are paired repeatedly with more tangible rewards, the words gradually become very powerful by themselves. However, for many small children in the early stages of learning, food may be the only powerful reinforcement available. The treat is divided into tiny portions so that the child does not get his fill too quickly and we vary the foods. We also use lavish praise that will gradually become rewarding for most children because it has been paired with the food.

Some parents ask if a child will gain weight under this approach. We have never seen it happen. The food is offered in tiny bites. In addition, contrary to the stereotype, we rarely use chocolate candies as a reward. Tastes of yogurt, pickles, olives, pretzels, and little chunks of apple are typical food rewards. Of course, each child's rewards must fit his or her preferences. If the food is not attractive, it will not be a reinforcement for the child and learning will not go well.

Tangible rewards such as food are gradually faded (phased out) over time so the child will not become dependent on them and will not expect them after each trial. For example, after some months of teaching the only food reward might be a snack at the end of a full lesson.

Another reward that is very potent for many children is allowing them to take a brief break after a little bit of work. For example, a child might be required to do one or two trials and then take a short play break. Gradually the number of trials be-

Figure 5-4

DOUGLASS SCHOOL

Educational Program Form

Student: Charlie Y   **School Year:** 96-97

Area: Social Skills   **Coordinator:** Emmet

Date Initiated: 1/97   **Date Mastered:** 3/97

Target Behavior: Engage in conversation with peers.

Behavioral Objective: Charlie, standing in circle of peers, will select a conversational card and have at least one thing to say about that topic. He will attend while others speak.

Description of Program: Establish group attention. At least 4 children in circle including Charlie.

Sd for Target Behavior: "It is conversation time. Charlie, please come up and choose a topic."

Consequence: Behavior specific praise.

Procedure:

1. Have each child stand in conversational circle
2. Place the interest cards around the circle
3. Explain the rules of the game. Tell the children they can take turns choosing an interest card. One child chooses a card and places it in their circle. When the card is in their circle that is the topic of conversation. Everyone in the conversation circle must talk about that topic. When the conversation is over or everyone has talked on the topic (encourage it to go as naturally as possible), the next child can pick an interest card.

Prompt Hierarchy: Initially Charlie should not be among first three children to take a turn choosing card. Gradually move him forward in the sequence. Whisper rules as needed.

Generalization: Charlie should be able to play Conversation Circle with any randomly selected group of 4 children in class.

Sets: Not applicable.

Materials:

1. Masking tape to make circles on floor large enough for each child in group. Circles should be large enough for each child

Figure 5-4 continued

to stand in and located appropriate distance from other circles.

2. 5 to 10 interest cards. Football, autumn leaves, super-heroes, etc.

Data: + = correct, - = incorrect, p= prompted. Collect as probe data.

Trials: Each child including Charlie should have at least 3 opportunities in a game.

Criterion: Follows all rules correctly without prompts on two successive days.

Program Comments: At least four children in group. Rotate group members. Vary the cards to ensure continuing interest.

fore a break is increased. For some children this reward is even more powerful than food.

What Does It Mean If a Child Does Not Make Progress?

Sometimes children fail to make progress on an ABA program. There can be several reasons for this. One is that the child is not motivated to do the work. In that case, it is important to consider using more powerful rewards. Another possibility is that the child has been asked to make too great a leap in learning. We may have left out some important intermediate skills. For example, if we are trying to teach a child to initiate a play interaction with another child, we would need to ensure that he knew how to play the game, knew how to say the words, and had an appropriate way of approaching the other child. Unless the prerequisite skills are in place, the child may not be able to fill in the gaps on his own. Sometimes we may have chosen the wrong learning modality for helping a child learn a task. For example, if the child is more of a visual than an auditory learner we may need to offer visual cues such as pictures to help him with a lesson.

There are a small minority of children whose learning is limited by severe mental retardation or because they have childhood disintegrative disorder or Rett's disorder. Although all children with autism can learn compliance, imitation, functional communication, and adaptive skills such as dressing, hygiene, or household routines, some children may not be able to master many social skills or verbal expressive language. These children may find the sheer intensity of the methods we have described to be very stressful because of their limited ability to master new skills. For these children, modifications would have to be made in the teaching approach. For example, modifications might include a more visually based curriculum, fewer language demands, a greater emphasis on self-help and daily living skills, and more frequent rewards.

Often it will take a skilled consultant to analyze why a child is not learning a lesson. Parents may develop that level of skill eventually, but it is a sophisticated assessment process that requires expertise.

What If My Child Won't Cooperate?

Noncompliance (uncooperative behavior) is often a problem in the early stages of teaching. One reason is that many children have learned that uncooperative behavior is a good way to get out of demands. In fact, some children will have significant temper tantrums in the early stages of learning. They have to learn that the rewards for cooperating are far greater than those for noncompliance. When noncompliance occurs later in teaching, it may signal the need for an adjustment in curriculum. Solving these problems is the role of your home consultant or your child's teacher. This kind of troubleshooting requires an intimate knowledge of a dynamic curriculum that can shift and change in response to the child's needs. Sometimes we may have made too great a leap for a child from one program to the next, and sometimes we may be asking a child to respond in a modality that is especially difficult for him.

How Does an ABA Curriculum Relate to the IFSP or IEP?

As Chapter 1 explains, children who receive any publically funded early intervention or special education services are required to have an IFSP (if under the age of 3) or an IEP (if over the age of 3). These documents list the short-term objectives and long-term goals that have been set for the child in each developmental area or academic subject in which he is experiencing difficulty. They also specify what services will be provided to help the child meet his goals and in what setting the services will be provided. The IEP and IFSP are frequently reviewed and modified to reflect the child's changing needs.

It should be easy to link your child's teaching programs to his or her IEP. Part of the strength of applied behavior analysis is that goals and objectives are specific and measurable. That kind of objectivity is also central to every IEP. In our work we often find school personnel receptive to incorporating our goals directly into the IEP or else attaching our plan to the IEP document with a note to see the attachment.

When more than one agency is providing services to your child, it is crucial that everyone is "reading from the same page." Although following the IEP helps in that regard, the IEP document itself does not have enough detail to ensure that different people are doing the same things. As a result, you as a parent or someone else involved in coordinating your child's education must ensure that everyone is using the same methods to reach goals. This collaborative approach is vital if your child is not to be confused and frustrated by having different people hold different expectations. At the Douglass School, we invite parents, outside professionals including members of the child study team, and our own staff to come together to discuss plans and agree on joint strategies. We have found that when we fail to do this it is the child who pays the price. If your child's program does not provide for these kinds of meetings you might ask staff to consider holding one. You may also invite the people who develop your child's ABA program to your child's IEP meeting with the school district.

In Sum

A comprehensive curriculum is a vital tool for any center-based or home-based program. This curriculum is the roadmap that helps teachers plan a child's instructional programs and move from one goal to the next. Not only should there be a well-ordered sequence of goals, but also instructional programs to support each goal. In addition to having access to a good curriculum, it is essential that the teacher be sufficiently experienced to know when to deviate from the curriculum and how to adapt the teaching programs to the needs of each child. The curriculum is not a cookbook, but a set of guidelines.

Parents Speak

Autism has put a hole in my heart that will never mend. It has ripped my heart apart in a way that is hard to repair. To watch my son struggle with life's simplest tasks can be overwhelming at times. Thinking of him in therapy for hours instead of playing with his friends or going to a movie is torture for me. But I know it's what is best for him and it's what he needs right now. Because of all the progress he has made, it makes it a bit easier to take. Will he ever be like other little boys? I don't know. I do know that I love him just the way he is and that he has taught me to be excited by things we take for granted each day. Each milestone he reaches I will be by his side to applaud him. I do believe in miracles and yes, maybe someday, I will dance with him at his wedding.

☙

The school has been great about teaching us how to understand what they are doing for our son. The home support consultant comes to see us every couple of weeks. She brings programs and shows us how to use them. She always asks us what we want and works with us to write the programs to help with problems around the house. For example, we wanted to find some way for our two-year-old to start to play with Jack. The consultant gave us a program that they both love.

૭ᖆ

The first time we visited they showed us this thick book full of programs and charts and said they had one for each child. I was really impressed because all of the goals and everything was so clear.

૭ᖆ

We did a home-based program for more than a year. Our consultant really knew what he was doing. He helped us plan step by step what to teach Sara. And he taught us the methods to use in teaching every program. What a blessing he was. We had to learn a lot, but we had a fabulous teacher.

૭ᖆ

We chose the school because our research led us to believe applied behavior analysis held the greatest hope for our son's progress. The school was the most rigorous in following ABA of all the schools we looked at. Some explained that they used a more "humane" approach, but we believed the most "humane" thing we could do for our son was to give him the best possible chance to progress. We liked the fact that the school is actively involved in research and is part of a major university.

૭ᖆ

We were convinced early on that ABA offered the best-documented, broadest-based improvement for kids with autism. Other approaches were more "seductive," but we wanted to give our son the best possible long-range chance for a full life.

We've been lucky in that we never had a major problem with a professional who was working with our son, probably due in part to doing homework up front before selecting the therapists and the programs.

References

Here are a couple of good guides to curricula for children with autism. By themselves, neither of these guides will enable you to educate a child, but used in conjunction with behavioral teaching skills they could be quite valuable in setting up a teaching program. Both references are based on years of work in nationally recognized programs. The first, by David Holmes and his colleagues, was written at the Eden Institute in Princeton, New Jersey. The second, by Raymond Romanczyk and his co-workers, was done in the Children's Unit for Treatment and Evaluation at SUNY/Binghamton. For more information you can contact either one directly.

Holmes, D. L., Cohen, M., Beck, P., & Sersen, S. (eds.). (1991). *Eden Institute curriculum series: Core, Vol. I.* Princeton, NJ: The Eden Press.
You can reach the Eden Press at One Logan Lane, Princeton, NJ 08540.

Romanczyk, R.G., Lockshin, S., & Matey, L. *The Individualized goal selection curriculum 1997 – Version 9.0.* Apalachin, NY: CBTA.
You can contact Dr. Romanczyk at the Department of Psychology, SUNY/Binghamton, Binghamton, NY 13902.

6 | How to Identify a Quality Program

The G Family Selects a Program

After Grace and Allan decided to enroll Tad in a center-based program, they visited three different programs in their area. One was a classroom for children with autism at the children's hospital, the second was located in a public school, and the third was a university-based school that had a specialized preschool for children with autism. There was another program in a nearby school district they wanted to visit because of its good reputation, but that school said they only accepted children whose parents lived in the district, and they did not offer tours to families from outside of the community. The Gs were to find that there were more families seeking placements than there were quality programs, and as a result they had to work hard to find the right match for Tad.

The Gs had received a checklist from their local autism society suggesting guidelines for parents in evaluating a program. They used this resource to assess each program they visited. The checklist helped them focus on items such as the number of children in the class, the number of adults in the classroom, the ability level of the children in the class where Tad might be placed, and so forth. During their interview with the program administrator, they explored such questions as the availability of a speech-language specialist, whether the program was open 12 months a year, and how the program helped children make the transition from their school to the next placement. The Gs planned to be very actively involved in Tad's education and they listened carefully to feel confident that the program would welcome their involvement and would teach them the skills they needed to work with him at home.

How Will You Approach Your Search?

It is very important to see personally the programs that may serve your child. A professional from your school district may make suggestions based on his or her experience in placing other children, and may wish to go with you on the visits. However, no amount of professional judgement can replace your own decision as a parent. Professionals are your consultants and your partners, not your boss! Grace and Allan visited each of the schools that had been suggested to them, and asked a series of questions to ensure they were satisfied with the resources that were available. Although they were always careful to be respectful of the program and not to appear critical in their evaluation, they were nonetheless asking for the information that would allow them to decide who could best serve Tad. When the director of one program appeared annoyed and resentful of their questions, they knew they could not obtain the parent-professional collaboration they were seeking from that program.

Choosing a Program

The program you select for your child can have a far-reaching impact on her welfare. In the previous chapters of this book we have touched on a variety of features you might hope to find in an educational program for a child with autism. This chapter brings that information together in a fashion that is convenient for you. Use the items in Table 6-1 as an outline to follow in organizing the information you collect about the programs you visit.

The Children and the Services

Who Is Served?

Look for a classroom that is designed specifically for children with autism. Some early intervention programs and pre-

Table 6-1 | Questions to Consider in Visiting a Program

The Children and the Services

- Who are the children in the program?
- What is the functioning level of the children?
- Does the program offer the services your child needs?
- How many hours of instruction are offered?
- Is the program year-round?
- How does the program support transition to new services?

Meeting the Unique Needs of Each Child

- Does the program follow the IFSP or IEP?
- How is the child's progress evaluated?
- Is the ratio of adults to children correct for your child?
- How do they manage behavior problems?

Home Support Services

- Will you be offered training in applied behavior analysis?
- Will staff members be available to help you develop home programs?
- Are parents and/or sibling support groups available?

Supervision and Accountability

- How are the staff members supervised?
- How do staff members stay up-to-date on teaching methods?
- Are staff members and students "on-target" most of the time?
- Is it clear who is in charge of the program?

school programs are called "generic" programs because they serve children with a range of disabilities. You might find children with attention deficit hyperactivity disorder, mental retardation, and autism in a single preschool class. That kind of mix is not typically in the best interests of a young child with autism, who needs very special and intensive educational services. Because the educational needs of children with autism are so highly specialized, it is unusual to find those resources offered in a classroom that serves a blend of children with various diagnoses. Other children may not need the intensity, the precise structure, or the great consistency in the use of applied behavior analysis that is so essential to children with autism.

Although there may be exceptions, most "generic" special education preschool classes will not have the teaching technology and staffing resources required by the young child with autism. In our opinion, a good home-based program or a class in another school district that offers specialized services will almost invariably be better for a child with autism than a generic preschool class. In a cooperative school district, you may be able to work closely with your district to create an appropriate program for children with autism. In an uncooperative district, you may need to assert your legal rights to get the services your child needs.

What is the Functioning Level of the Children?

Look for a classroom in which the children are roughly comparable to your child. There will certainly be variation among children, but you want your child to be with others whose needs are similar and who can provide appropriate stimulation. If your child's skills are markedly superior to every other child in the class he might be a fine model for them, but he would probably lack models for himself.

What Kind of Support Services Does Your Child Require?

Look for a classroom that has the specialized support services your child needs. It would be a cause for serious concern if the class did not have the extensive services of a speech-language specialist and of a psychologist to consult on behavior problems. In addition, some children need additional service such as physical therapy. Does the program offer those services? If not, can you arrange to have them provided before or after school in another setting? For example, at the Douglass School we do not have physical therapy or occupational therapy. Parents who wish to obtain these services for their child schedule them after school.

We have found school districts to be very cooperative in making these arrangements. It would not be unusual for a small program that specialized in treating children with autism not to have their own physical therapist or adaptive physical education specialist. However, if your child needs that service, or any other, you will want to be certain it is part of his educational plan.

How Many Hours of Instruction Will Your Child Receive?

Look for a program that offers five days a week of full-day instruction. Young children with autism need an intensive educational experience if they are to make optimal progress. A couple of hours a day, one or two days a week will not do the job. As explained in the discussion of the work of Ivar Lovaas in Chapter 2, those children in the 10-hour-a-week program did not make much progress, while nearly half of those in the 40-hour-a-week program did very well. The program you are evaluating may not offer 40 hours a week of instruction, but they should be prepared to work with you to help you supplement that instruction to bring it up to 40 hours. At the Douglass School we provide 25 hours a week of teaching in school and expect parents to supplement that with 15 hours a week at home. We give parents the written home programs and support they need to carry out that home instruction.

Is It A Year Round Program?

Look for a program that is open all year. Summer vacation is a lot of fun for typically developing children, but often a burden for children with autism. They cannot afford to take the summer "off." Children with autism seem to be especially vulnerable to losing hard-won ground over a prolonged summer break. Although most programs do close for vacation periods, it is probably better to have these breaks scattered through the year and not taken in a long chunk over the summer.

What Happens When Your Child Graduates from the Specialized Placement?

Quality programs always have specific procedures they use to follow up on a child's progress after she graduates from the services of that center. For example, at the Douglass School, a member of our staff is available to visit the child in the new placement and to consult with the new teacher about programming concerns. We find that many schools are very receptive to this continuing consultation, while a few reject our offer of help. After the new placement has been identified, we visit with the parents and personnel from the school district, talk with the new teacher and invite him or her to come to our program, and collaborate with the future placement in making a gradual transition from one setting to the next. Typically, one of our staff members goes with the child during these transition visits. That allows us to support the child in her efforts to adapt to the new class, and to teach the child new skills that may be essential to the move.

Meeting the Unique Needs of Your Child

Does the Program Follow a Child's Educational Plan?

Look for a program in which instruction is linked to the child's educational plan. Every child should have either an Individualized Family Service Plan (IFSP) or an Individualized Educational Program (IEP). The IFSP is used in early intervention programs for children under the age of 3 years, while the IEP is used for children enrolled in preschool or school-age programs. In either case, this plan is the road map for your child's education. It describes the goals of the educational program and the means to be used to achieve those goals. These goals should be written in behavior-specific language that clearly defines the desired skills and allows skill acquisition to be measured. For example, the goal "Relates to other children" is vague and hard to measure. If the IEP said, "John will approach another child and invite that child to play a game of catch" that would be specific and measurable. You have the right to be an active participant in the development of your child's plan, and you should not accept a plan unless you agree with it.

How Is a Child's Progress Evaluated?

Look for a program that keeps careful records on each child's progress. A quality program that uses behavioral technology for educating children with autism will keep careful records of children's progress. Sometimes these records may be what we call "trial by trial data." Trial by trial record keeping involves recording whether each response by a child was correct and whether or not he or she needed help (a prompt) to complete a task. Another method of record keeping is to collect "probes" on a child's performance. Rather than taking the time to make a record of performance after each response, when probes are used the teacher sets aside a block of time once every few days to record progress. For example, on Friday afternoon she might collect probe data on the several programs she is using with a child. If she believes he has mastered a program sooner, she could do a probe at any time she wished.

Data collected about a child's performance should be kept in an organized fashion. Often the data is recorded on a graph so that it is possible to track the child's progress visually. In quality programs, data is not only kept, but used. Decisions about when to change programs and whether or not a child is making progress should always be based on data.

The graph in Figure 6-1 shows information about Paul, a little boy with autism who had many fine skills, but whose aggression kept him from being with other children. We addressed this behavior with a combination of special rewards for times when he was not aggressive and having him sit quietly at the edge of the classroom and watch his classmates for two minutes after an episode of attempted aggression. This "time-out" procedure only works when a child likes the activities of the classroom enough to dislike being removed. Some children enjoy time-out and will actually increase their problematic behavior so they can escape from class!

The graph in Figure 6-1 shows the changes in Paul's aggression over several months. When he entered the class in September, we collected baseline (pretreatment) data by counting the

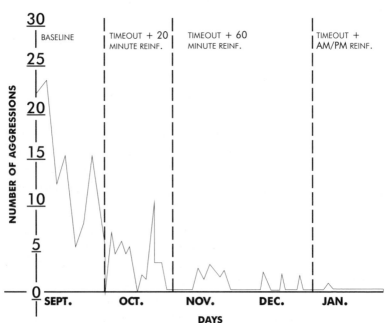

Figure 6-1: Paul's Aggressive Behavior

number of times Paul tried to be aggressive. We did not begin to treat the aggression until we had those baseline data. In October we introduced the treatment procedures by rewarding Paul after every 20 minutes without an aggressive episode and using the timeout when he attempted to be aggressive. Because he responded so well, in November we thinned the special reward schedule to once an hour, and in January he was given the special reward once in the morning and once in the afternoon. Notice how quickly Paul's behavior improved when we started the procedures. By keeping the graph, we could track Paul's behavior and be certain his misbehavior remained at suitably low levels for several months. If we had not seen these encouraging changes we would have tried other procedures to help him learn self-control.

What Is the Staff Ratio?

Look for a program that has enough adults to meet the needs of your child. Most very young children with autism who are just starting an instructional program require a one-to-one ratio most of the time. Other children who have mastered some of the basic skills will be better off with somewhat less intense teaching because they need to learn how to share a teacher's time, learn in a group, and do independent work. It is important that the classroom have enough well-trained staff to meet the needs of your child.

How Does the Program Manage Behavior Problems?

Children with autism often engage in behaviors that may intrude on their learning. These can include tantrums, aggression, or self-stimulatory (stereotyped behavior) such as rocking or hand waving. Although an occasional preschool child may demonstrate serious self-injury such as damaging head banging, usually behavior management problems in very young children are not so strongly entrenched nor so dangerous that strongly aversive (punishing) procedures are needed to control them. The case of Paul described above is a good example of the benefits of an effective reward combined with a very mild punishment.

Those of us who specialize in the treatment of children with autism have available a very effective technology for evaluating the causes of disruptive behavior and for teaching children more appropriate alternatives. The use of this technology, called "functional assessment," involves observing the child under various conditions to identify the circumstances under which the behavior is most likely to occur. After the observations have been analyzed and the conditions defined, it is often possible to teach the child another way to achieve a desired outcome. For example, a child who throws tantrums to get out of work can be taught to ask for a short break from that work.

You will want to know how any program you are considering deals with disruptive or dangerous behaviors. If your child poses a problem behavior, they should do a functional assessment of her behavior, and select the least intrusive treatment necessary to help her learn to control the behavior. Unless your child engages in very dangerous behavior, be quite skeptical of a program that wants to use a substantial aversive.

Often very mild but consistent consequences such as ignoring unwanted behavior while offering generous praise for appropriate behavior is all it takes to help a young child understand that a behavior is unacceptable. When those methods fail, we try using a mild consequence such as saying a firm "No," holding a child's hands down for a brief moment, or briefly withdrawing attention (sometimes called "time-out") to teach the child self-control. Any of those methods would be used in conjunction with a great deal of reinforcement for appropriate behavior. Remember, however: there is nothing "cookbook" about these methods and even when these mild treatments are used, an appropriate functional assessment must be completed to ensure we are targeting the correct problem.

Mild consequences are usually sufficient to help most very young children learn not to engage in problematic behavior. However, if your child has more severe behavior problems, you will want to be certain the program you select has the professional expertise to deal with these problems. Also be certain that you are fully informed of the procedures that they use with your child, and that the procedures are coordinated with you at home.

Whenever we use a procedure to decrease an unwanted behavior at the Douglass School, we provide the parents with a written description of the behavior and the procedures we plan to use to address it. That holds true even for very mild procedures like holding a child's hands on the desk for a few seconds. No procedure is put into effect until the parents agree to it. Should they disagree with our recommendations, we meet with them to develop a plan that has everyone's approval.

Home Support Resources

Are Parents Offered Training in the Program's Teaching Methods?

A great deal of research documents that it is very important to the progress of the child with autism that parents support the efforts of the school. Consistency from one setting to another is essential in ensuring that your child makes the best progress possible. This consistency is important to helping your child transfer newly learned skills from the school to other settings. This process of transfer is sometimes called "generalization," a term which

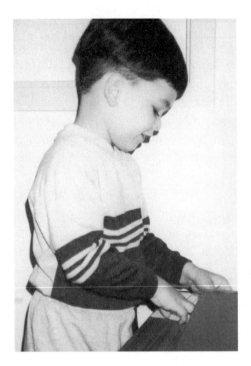

refers to the notion that skills learned in one setting with one teacher should be able to be used in many settings with many different people. Research also shows that parents can master any of the teaching skills used in the classroom. The experience of parents who rely on home-based instruction demonstrates that parents can become highly skilled in the use of behavioral teaching methods. A quality program should offer you the opportunity to learn about the teaching methods that are employed in the school and help you reach a level of proficiency that will enable you to do home programming with your child.

Are Staff Members Available to Visit Your Home on a Regular Basis?

Although some centers provide home programming only through visits to the center by the parents, many quality programs send a staff member to the home to consult. This consultation includes help in designing programs to address specific problems at home as well as help to ensure a smooth transfer of programs being done in the school to the home.

Does the Program Provide Parent and/or Sibling Support Groups?

Raising a child with autism is a very stressful experience that has an impact on parents and siblings alike. Family members are often called upon to sacrifice time, privacy, emotional energy, and control over their lives, which can result in significant stress. Parents at the Douglass School tell me that no one understands that stress better than another parent who has been down the same road. Recognizing the existence of this stress and the potential benefits of mutual support, many quality programs offer parent support groups, and some also offer sibling support groups. These groups give members a safe place in which to reflect on the experience of raising a child with autism, share coping strategies, and offer one another the mutual respect and caring that makes it easier to manage in the face of stress.

If the program in which your child is enrolled does not offer support groups or if you have a home-based program, you may want to consider seeking a group elsewhere. For example, some state chapters of the Autism Society of America provide this service to their members.

Supervision and Accountability

How Are Teachers Supervised?

No matter how experienced and skilled a teacher may be, it is valuable to have periodic supervision available. For younger, less experienced team members, this supervision is vital. The program should provide for periodic observation by the supervisor of the staff members working with children. Teachers should be meeting on a regular basis with a senior supervisor to review treatment plans and to receive feedback about their work. The teachers, in turn, should offer regular feedback to their classroom assistants about their work. Unless we are supervised we tend to repeat the same mistake again and again. Even an experienced, highly skilled person can fall into bad habits. We can all benefit from feedback. That holds true for you as a parent working with your child as well. Be certain to ask for periodic feedback on your teaching skills from your home support staff member, your child's teacher, or someone else who is knowledgeable.

It is important that feedback be given in an open and constructive fashion. There is an art to helping people grow in their skills. An important aspect of that art is creating an atmosphere in which the person being supervised feels respected and valued for what she has achieved and challenged to continue to grow. Staff members who feel threatened by the supervision process are less likely to be open to learning and trying new methods and more likely to try to avoid their supervisors!

Are Staff Up-to-Date on Teaching Methods?

Behavioral teaching methods for working with children with autism have changed radically in the past ten years. A program that relied on methods that were in use ten years ago would be out of date today. How does the program you are considering ensure that teachers and other staff are able to keep current on teaching methods? One approach is through in-service training, in which a consultant provides training at the school for staff. Another approach is to send staff to professional conferences on the treatment of autism. There are many conferences every year at which experts on autism discuss current teaching methods. Staff should be encouraged to attend these meetings and to transfer the skills to their own work. The center should also provide staff with access to current journals and books about teaching methods.

Are Staff and Children "On Target" Most of the Time?

Refer to a copy of the class schedule while you are observing. Are staff following the teaching programs? Are they adhering to the classroom schedule? Is most of the time spent in active teaching? Teachers should organize materials ahead of time and be familiar with a child's programs. Minimal time should be spent between programs. Teachers should not be smoking, chatting with one another, drinking coffee, and so forth. Their task is to be focused on the children. This is not to suggest that there should be no moments of conversation, or that things do not sometimes get off schedule. Children are unpredictable, and sometimes flexibility is necessary to meet their needs. However, most of the teaching day staff should be on schedule and on task. An excess of down time suggests a failure to be properly organized.

Who is Responsible?

Does the program have a clear chain of command? Do you know who works with the children? Who supervises that individual? Who is the administrator who runs the program? Can you have access to that administrator if you need to? It should be clear to parents and staff alike who is in charge.

In Sum

You need to ask hard questions when you select a program for your child. Although no program is perfect, there are some excellent resources available for the education of children with autism. Visit each program with a list of items that you want to observe. As you watch the classroom in action, some of the information you need may become obvious. Other information can be learned during your interview with a senior administrator. Don't feel shy about asking what you need to know. At the Douglass Center, we are not surprised when parents pull out a list of questions during a meeting so they can check to see if they have addressed all the points they wanted to cover. We think that's a smart idea, and we are not at all offended by it. We may not give them an ideal answer to every question, but we can discuss their concerns, and they can be certain they know what our program has to offer their child.

Parents Speak

My son's teacher and her assistants are very caring and dedicated individuals. We are all working together to see that he reaches his full potential. It is so important that everyone involved is working toward a common goal. All lines of communication should be open between home and school. In addition to school, my son still has 12 hours of home therapy a week and my home coordinator is also in touch with his teacher. They work together to try to solve any existing problems. My son is blessed to have such a dynamic team of people working for him. I too am in daily contact with my son's teacher. I know the programs he is working on and I carry it all out at home whenever possible. What's taught at school must be done at home to be successful.

☾☽

We visited three different programs that spring before Dylan started school. You learn a lot if you keep your mouth shut and just watch for a while. We saw one teacher who always had a sour look on her face and her assistants didn't look too happy either. In another place, everyone was warm and seemed happy. They both used applied behavior analysis, but the atmosphere was so very different.

☾☽

Be sure to tell other parents to take a list of questions with them. I always got kind of nervous when we were in the school and it helped to have my list so I knew I didn't forget anything. Nobody seemed to mind. I liked feeling free to call back if we did have questions.

☾☽

His progress is not so much miraculous, but no less a gift from God. We have been richly blessed with the best of services and support from a long list of professional people who have helped us to help our son. Everyone from diagnosticians, to therapists, to educators, was the very best. We have witnessed the adaptation and guided the development of his autistic brain into one that maintains only a subtle shadow of autism. The gifts of the science of Dr. Lovaas, applied behavior analysis, and the Douglass Programs are the miracles that produced this success; along with, of course, our son's own persistent and determined spirit.

APPENDIX

Resources for Further Information

There are two resources you can check that will connect you to many others.

1. If you have access to the Internet, take a look at a site called **Autism Resources** created by John Wobus. Through this site you can find the Internet address of nearly every autism-related site we know of. The address is *<web.syr.edu/~jmwobus/autism/index.html>*.

2. The **Autism Society of America** has both a fine home page and material they can mail you (via good old snail mail!). You will find lots of information for new parents, membership information, help in finding your local chapter, etc. Their address is:

>   Autism Society of America
>   7910 Woodmont Avenue, Suite 650
>   Bethesda, MD 20814-3015
>   800-328-8476; 301-657-0869 (fax)
>   Web site: http://www.autism-society.org

3. If you become really involved in ABA, you may be interested in the annual meeting of the **Association for Behavior Analysis.** Top people in the field assemble there to report on current research. However, unlike the annual convention of the Autism Society of America, which is oriented toward families, this is a meeting for professionals, so expect a lot of debate about the details of research. Their home address is:

Association for Behavior Analysis
213 West Hall
Western Michigan University
1201 Oliver St.
Kalamazoo, MI 49008
616-387-8341; 616-387-8354 (fax)
Web site:
http://www.wmich.edu/aba/contents.html

A note of caution: Anyone can create a web page. The material you find on the Internet may or may not be accurate. Although there is a great deal of useful information in cyberspace, there is also some baloney. Use very good judgement!

INDEX

About the Authors

Sandra L. Harris, Ph.D., is Professor and Dean of the Graduate School of Applied and Professional Psychology at Rutgers, The State University of New Jersey. She is also the author of *SIBLINGS OF CHILDREN WITH AUTISM* (Woodbine House, 1994) and the Executive Director of the Douglass Developmental Disabilities Center, a program for children and adolescents with autism, which she founded in 1972.

Mary Jane Weiss, Ph.D., is a research assistant professor, also at Rutgers. She is Director of the Rutgers Autism Program and Division Director for the Research and Training Division at the Douglass Developmental Disabilities Center.